THE

NOTES

including
- *Life and Background*
- *List of Characters*
- *Introduction to the Novel*
- *Critical Commentaries*
- *Structural Devices*
- *Motifs*
- *Study Questions*
- *Theme Topics*
- *Selected Bibliography*

by
Edward A. Kopper, Jr., Ph.D.
Professor of English
Slippery Rock State College

INCORPORATED
LINCOLN, NEBRASKA   68501

Editor

Gary Carey, M.A.
University of Colorado

Consulting Editor

James L. Roberts, Ph.D.
Department of English
University of Nebraska

ISBN 0-8220-1071-2
© Copyright 1986
by
C. K. Hillegass
All Rights Reserved
Printed in U.S.A.

Cliffs Notes, Inc.   Lincoln, Nebraska

CONTENTS

MOTIFS

THE POWER AND THE GLORY
Notes

LIFE AND BACKGROUND

Graham Greene describes his boyhood traumas in *A Sort of Life* (1971), the first volume of his autobiography. He was born in 1904, attended a public school, of which his father was headmaster, and later he studied at Oxford. The unhappiness of his home and school life led him to attempt suicide through a variation of Russian roulette and brought about his treatment by a psychoanalyst.

Graham became a Catholic in 1926, his faith stemming in part from his deep conviction of evil in the world. Much of his life up to that point had been a nightmare, and no doubt because he has long kept dream journals, many of the characters in his novels incur horrifying dreams. The novels also reflect Greene's experiences with the seamy side of life. His protagonists' experiences, for example, often parallel his labors as a journalist (for a Nottingham paper), his government work, and his travels through totalitarian Mexico.

Greene maintains that his works fall into two categories, novels and "entertainments," though often the latter are quite serious in parts. *The Honorary Consul* (1973) is "entertaining," but it is also a profound view of terrorism and the military state in Argentina. Greene's novels are frequently characterized by their focus on (1) a hunted man as the protagonist; on (2) the discrepancy between the outer man and the inner man – in fact, his first novel is entitled *The Man Within* (1929); on (3) multi points-of-view and vivid metaphysical detail; and (4) on a nineteenth-century method of storytelling which is more reminiscent of Robert Louis Stevenson than, say, of a modern writer such as James Joyce. Setting also plays a pronounced role in Greene's novels, whether it is an abandoned section of Africa, as in *The Heart of the Matter* (1948), or a leper colony, as in *A Burnt-Out Case* (1961).

Many of his works focus upon religious themes, and the protagonist is almost always the sinner, the spiritual outcast. Greene's milieu is the fallen world, and he has been criticized for focusing on the eccentric believer, rather than on the conventional believer, and for combining theological strictures with somewhat lurid, perhaps overly personal, views of sex. *The End of the Affair* (1951), for example, is as much a study of hate as it is a study of triangular love.

One key source of background information for *The Power and the Glory* is Greene's *The Lawless Roads* (1939), a book which describes his travels of the previous year through the Mexican provinces of Tabasco and Chiapas, where the events of this novel take place. The major characters in *The Power and the Glory* originate in people whom Greene met or heard about in his journey through these two totalitarian states.

The second volume of Greene's autobiography, *Ways of Escape*, was published in 1980.

LIST OF CHARACTERS

Anita

A dead five-year-old girl, at whose grave Padre José refuses to pray.

Beckley, Henry

The director of the correspondence school who sends Coral Fellows packets of school lessons that are far more elementary than her chronological potential.

Brigitta

The illegitimate daughter of the fugitive priest-protagonist.

Calver, James

An American bank robber and murderer pursued by the Mexican police throughout the novel; he is finally killed.

Father _____

'The new priest who arrives at the end of the novel to replace the executed priest-protagonist.

Fellows, Captain Charles

The operator of the Central American Banana Company.

Fellows, Coral

The Fellowses' precocious daughter.

Fellows, Mrs. Trix (Trixy)

Fellows' wife.

The Half-Caste

A mestizo; the Judas who betrays the priest.

An Indian Woman

Her child is shot by either Calver or by the soldiers who are pursuing Calver.

The Jefe

The lieutenant's superior.

Mr. Lehr

A Protestant living in one of the less vehemently anti-religious Mexican states.

Miss Lehr

His shortsighted sister.

The Lieutenant

Out of a sense of duty, he stalks the priest-protagonist from the beginning of the novel until its end; finally he captures him.

Lopez

A hostage who was executed (before the action of the novel begins) for helping priests escape.

Luis

A fourteen-year-old Mexican boy; he rebels against the sentimentality of his mother's stories about young Juan.

Luis' Father

A cynical, disillusioned man who believes that his wife's Catholic faith is futile, naive folly.

Luis' Mother

She fervently and dramatically reads to Luis and his two sisters from the Holy Book.

Maria

The mother of Brigitta, the priest-protagonist's daughter.

Miguel

He is taken as a hostage and is beaten by the police.

Montez, Pedro

The hostage killed at Concepción; the priest-protagonist calls himself "Montez" afterward.

Padre José

He is a priest who was forced to marry by state regulations and, thus, he was excommunicated.

Padre José's Wife

A fat and bossy shrew.

The Priest (alias Montez)

The protagonist, or main character of the novel; the only active priest still in Mexico.

A Pious Woman

She condemns the priest-protagonist for his bad spirituality during their night in jail.

Mr. Tench

A dentist who is trapped in Mexico because of the economy.

Tench, Sylvia

His estranged wife.

Young Juan

A perfect little boy in a religious story, who will become, we assume, a "plaster saint." Luis' mother reads stories in the Holy Book about him to her children.

INTRODUCTION TO THE NOVEL

In *The Power and the Glory*, Greene examines the bases of sin and salvation by focusing on the final months in the life of a man who is the last priest still practicing his calling in Mexico. In his treatment of the fugitive, Greene offers two possible views of the protagonist's plight, and he allows his readers to form their own conclusions concerning the priest's fate in eternity.

The first view sees the priest's holiness as almost a truism. The clergyman has lived in the most dire conditions for years in Mexico – half-starved, assaulted by fever and the police – simply to carry out God's will. Even his death is caused by his sense of duty: he *could* have stayed across the mountains in safety, but he chose instead to administer Last Rites to the dying outlaw, Calver, although he sensed that he would be wasting his time and that the message summoning him was almost assuredly a police trick. We discover, however, that Calver *did* write the note.

The second view is expressed by the pious woman incarcerated with the priest. She condemns him. In her eyes, the priest is merely a drunk, a lecher, a jester at Church precepts, and, above all, a sinner who will not repent.

The novel alternates between these two positions, focusing on the priest's own ruminations concerning the state of his soul. Greene has chosen a most complex man to carry the burden of his theological ideas. But the priest has the capacity – and the opportunity – to analyze theological problems that have always troubled humankind.

The nameless priest becomes Everyman, picking his way through the labyrinths of Mexico's mountain ranges and swamps in his attempt to do God's will, even though his spiritual situation is unnecessarily complicated by issues that would bother no one but the priest himself.

Greene's priest has a tender conscience and a tendency to see *only* the evil in his actions and to exaggerate his blemishes. To such a man, virtues become vices and, added to valid guilt, they almost overpower him. Greene's priest, however, *does* have reason to repent. He was pompous in the early days of his priesthood; he subjugated emotions and concern for others to intellectual gymnastics; he did commit adultery; and he does drink far too much and might well be an alcoholic.

But his *imagined* crimes, he feels, are much worse. He feels guilty because he loves the offspring of his sin, Brigitta; he suspects that his refusal to leave Mexico stems merely from pride; he broods over taking a lump of sugar from a dead child and snatching a bone from a dying dog – even though he himself is starving. He concerns himself unduly for enjoying a few days of rest at the Lehrs' home, and while there, he is immediately conscious of his tendency to return to his old, stilted ways, so sensitized is his conscience to any possible rumblings of sin.

The priest, then, is a fully drawn character; but he is also a spokesman for Greene's view of the continuity of the Catholic Church. As a sensitive and thoughtful person, the protagonist is scarcely expendable; yet he is only a small part of a large spiritual organization – the Roman Catholic Church. In his debate with the lieutenant, the priest states that the totalitarian state is based upon personalities. When its leaders die, he says, the government will probably fall, consumed by corruption. The Church, he argues, does *not* depend on any one person, and the appearance of the new priest at the end of the novel manifests Greene's thesis.

But even the Church must work through people, and the novel traces the protagonist's growing awareness of the need for *compassion* and *acceptance* of the faults of others. Without charity (benevolence and loving forebearance), the Church would be as cold and as brittle as the totalitarian state. The lieutenant can erase caricatures from the walls that might ridicule the government, but the Church must be more tolerant, while all the time retaining its sanctifying missions. Starting with his dreadful night in the jail cell and ending with his kindness to the half-caste as they approach Calver, the priest's quest has been an effort to become totally human.

CRITICAL COMMENTARIES

PART ONE

Chapter 1: *The Port*

The first chapter of *The Power and the Glory* centers upon the meeting between Mr. Tench, the English dentist who is living in Mexico, and the priest-protagonist, who presents himself to Tench as a "quack." The priest secretly plans to escape further religious persecution by sailing to Vera Cruz (a Mexican seaport city) on the *General Obregon,* which is harbored at the quay, even though he is told by Tench that a man named Lopez, who has helped other priests escape, was shot by the police some weeks ago.

Tench and the priest then retreat to Tench's office, where they drink brandy together. They are interrupted by a boy (later, we discover that he is Luis, a Mexican boy who will play a key, symbolic role in the novel) who says that his mother is dying and that she needs a doctor (obviously a euphemism for a priest, who can administer Last Rites to the dying). The priest follows the boy, and in the distance, the *General Obregon* pulls away from the river bank. By chance, the priest inadvertently leaves his breviary behind, disguised inside the covers of a sleazy novel, *La Eterna Mártir.*

One of the first things one should notice in this first chapter are Greene's many references to decay; they prefigure symbolism which will occur throughout the rest of the book. For example, consider the thirty-yard-long *General Obregon*. It looks as if it will soon sink; at best, the ship will probably survive no more than two or three years, or less if she meets a severe storm. Her leaving on time is thoroughly *un*expected.

Moreover, Tench's first memory is of a discarded clay cast of a mouth, thrown away by his dentist-father into a wastebasket; Tench's life is "rootless," as he readily admits, remarking that in his profession, he "cast[s] in sand," and, thus, not surprisingly, when he takes down two glasses for the brandy, he must wipe sand out of them.

As Tench walks down toward the dock to see whether or not his ether cylinder, with its symbolic sleep-inducing gas, has arrived, he is shaken with nausea and frequently forgets the purpose of his errand. Tench is constantly clearing phlegm from his throat and spitting bile into the blank and melancholy streets. His days are futile, for no one will come to his dentist's parlor before five o'clock, and his advice to the priest is as worthless as his dentistry practice.

Tench's decay, however, is only a small part of the disintegration of a self-important historical movement in a totalitarian state which is continually being absorbed into history. The more pompous the Red Shirts become, the more ephemeral their state seems. Sentries either sit sleeping or glare silently beside walls and empty crates; the statues of dead generals are already mildewing; the water causes dysentery; in the rainy season, the village is engulfed in mud, and then the sun turns the streets into long strips of searing stone for the barefooted peasants.

Disarmingly, just as we applaud the priest's hopefully life-giving decision to go to the sick woman, an act which symbolically surpasses the sterile ethic of the Mexican state, we discover that the roots of the disreputable Tench go even deeper than those of the Mexican Red Shirt zealots. Tench's dentist-father's cast of a mouth set in clay resembles an archeological discovery unearthed in Dorset, perhaps Neanderthal or Pithecanthropus, and as he stands in his workshop, he is described as a benighted and confused caveman among fossils. Even the priest, too, in Greene's description, takes on a totemic importance – in his case, that of a West African king, one who is virtually indentured to his tribe.

Greene's abundant animal imagery in this chapter correlates the central image of decay with pictures of other types of decay. There are buzzards, turkeys pompously strutting around, hungry sharks just offshore, and ants which crawl like disciplined soldiers through the priest's spilled brandy.

As the buzzards flap overhead, they foreshadow – literally as well as symbolically – the death that will soon blacken the peace of this tiny plaza. One of these relentless creatures is seen as the black hand of a clock; another, as a cold, impartial observer. The deceiving buzzards resemble domesticated fowls, but, like their counterparts among the Mexican leaders, they are really parasites.

Few spots of real worth remain in this world of false values and artificiality. No one cares if the *General Obregon* sinks, since all the passengers are insured. Tench lies to a customs official, promising to have the officer's set of false teeth ready by nightfall. He takes pride in his battered-up dentistry shop. When the priest states that at least Mexico had God before the Red Shirts, Tench answers, "There's no difference in the teeth." To Tench, money is all-important, a cash down payment for promised dental work.

None of the characters in the novel is morally fit to receive the Eucharist, and, accordingly, allusions to physical mouths and teeth throughout the book suggest the characters' spiritual corruption. Even the priest's teeth are carious since he too is spiritually unfit for the Sacrament. Later, Greene calls attention to the "fangs" of the half-caste and to the police chief's swollen jaw. In addition, Tench's mouth frequently hangs open.

Tench and the priest are more similar than would at first be supposed. The men meet as Tench ogles a girl aboard the *General Obregon*, and, although the priest censoriously points out the girl's youth to Tench, he too is sinful, having committed, while a priest, an illicit sex act with Maria.

In Tench's shop, the dentist plays the symbolic part of the Mass celebrant. He pours the "wine" and urges the priest to "drink up" – that is, to receive. As the priest sips the brandy, the drink is like an "indulgence," a gift of God's grace. In a turnabout of roles, the priest asks Tench for advice about whether or not to accompany young Luis to the boy's dying mother.

The priest's spiritual death, from which he must resurrect himself in the novel, is perhaps best represented by his deathlike appearance. The disheveled, gaunt, unshaven little man, carrying a small attache case and a breviary hidden under the covers of a pornographic book, wears a suit which suggests a coffin to Tench. The priest is a mystery, a question mark, and, above all, a hollow man.

La Eterna Mártir, the title of the pornographic book, suggests the priest's resemblance to the cruel lover at whose feet the Edwardian woman crawls and begs. At present, the priest cannot accept Maria *or* his own daughter because she was conceived in sin.

Another feature of this chapter concerns the exposition, which is provided in a dialogue between Tench and the priest. In answer to the taciturn stranger's question, Tench explains that the *General Obregon* is bound for Vera Cruz; consider, at this time, that, symbolically, the priest's "true cross" (his *vera cruz*) is still to be found in the aggressively anti-Catholic Mexican state *if* he is to spiritually resurrect himself. The city of Vera Cruz is safer for priests than this village is, but an escape to safety would prevent the priest from progressing spiritually. Tench, of course, does not know that the priest *is* a priest; all he knows is that the man has said that he was a "quack" and that he inquired about the destination of the *General Obregon.* Thus, Tench says, without realizing the impact it will have on the priest, that Lopez, the man whom the priest inquired about, was shot by the police some time ago for helping "undesirables" (meaning priests) escape from the country.

Tench does not realize that the darkly dressed stranger cannot leave the country easily. He assumes that the stranger doesn't have his capital tied up in this part of Mexico, but remember that Tench doesn't know that a priest's "capital" is found in the souls of his countrymen.

Chapter 2: *The Capital*

In this chapter, the Chief of Police (the jefe) informs the lieutenant that he has heard that there is still a priest practicing in Mexico and that this priest attempted to "get away last week to Vera Cruz." The pink and flabby jefe complains that the Governor is pressuring him to capture the priest, although he has no idea what he looks like, and the only photograph of him is one taken years before at a First Communion party.

The lieutenant looks at the aged newspaper photo of the youngish priest, looking plump and harmless, and then he contrasts it with a picture of the bank robber and murderer James Calver, a "true man" in the lieutenant's eyes. The lieutenant, of course, does not realize that the priest has undergone a dramatic physical change since his days as pastor of Concepción.

Meanwhile, young Luis' mother (now recovered) reads a pious book to her family and expresses disgust when Luis questions her about Padre José, the priest who disgraced himself by marrying to escape persecution. She feels more kindly about the priest who came to her while she was ill—the one who, according to the smallest daughter, "smelt funny." Without a doubt, the priest-protagonist is a "whiskey priest"—that is, an alcoholic.

About this same time, in another part of town, Padre José, a fat, disillusioned man, a married priest, is called to bed by his nagging, overbearing wife. And he is also mocked unmercifully by the neighbor children outside, imitating perfectly the nasal whine of Padre José's wife.

Note also in this chapter that the lieutenant, who gazes with dislike at the newspaper photograph of the priest, shares several attributes of this very priest whom he will soon be hunting. The lieutenant's unwilling and ragged soldiers are members of *his* "parish," the parish to which he is inescapably chained, and note that he walks disdainfully ahead of his sloppily attired and ill-disciplined men. In another parallel, like the priest's clothes in Concepción, the officer's crisp, neat uniform distinguishes him from the rabble. Also, the lieutenant is as fanatical as an ardent theologian would be: he feels that he could easily sacrifice sex in order to build a perfect state. Indeed, says Greene, there is "something of a priest in his intent observant walk."

But the lieutenant's religion is one of vacuity, and, when he looks beyond the evidence of his senses, he pictures the peaceful cold of outer space. His theology reflects the Darwinian theory of evolution, but he brings to it his own brand of nihilism. To the lieutenant, the world is a cold, broken piece of earth which is populated with beings who have evolved from animals for no ultimate purpose at all.

The lieutenant has been deeply influenced by the deprivations of his childhood; the scar on his face and his crooked nose reflect close "escapes," both symbolic and actual. His "religion"—that is, his code of behavior—is spare, menacing, and well-honed, and it reflects his desire to cut from the body politic the institutions that caused him (as a child) and other children much pain. His lean, dancer-like body and his neatness mirror his ardent, almost religious desire to purge the "dross" elements of religion from Mexico. This dapper officer is in direct contrast to his slovenly superior, the jefe.

The jefe, the Chief of Police, is an awkward, flabby, uncommitted bureaucrat, a man who is more concerned with having his tooth extracted or filled than with ridding Mexico of its "last priest." He possesses a tolerance and a passivity that evade his subordinate, the lieutenant. The Chief of Police shares traits with the fat, ineffectual Padre José, and he also shares traits with the fatalistic father of young Luis. But the jefe is dangerous, for he simply carries out orders of his superiors – without demur or judgment.

Insights are rare for the Chief of Police, but once in awhile he does reveal a wisdom which shows him to be very much a part of the old, folk-oriented Mexico. For example, he finds some virtue in this "last priest," whom he calls "devilishly cunning" to escape capture for years.

Usually, the Chief of Police plays the buffoon. When he reaches into his pocket to find a pain alleviator for his toothache, his holster gets in the way. In the new, sterile state of Mexico, the jefe remains the stereotype of the ineffectual police officer often portrayed in American movies about Mexico. Thus, the lieutenant's task is a nearly impossible one, for incompetence and corruption are always above him in rank, as well as below him.

The lieutenant's "religion" is ephemeral, and this chapter symbolically shows the beginning erosion of the Mexican totalitarian state: plaster chips from walls expose mud; the soldiers are undisciplined and lazy despite the zeal of their leader; the life of the "liberated" peasant is sterile; and at 9:30 each night, the lights in the plaza go out. Even the children's swings are like gallows on the site of the cathedral.

Antagonism to the anti-religious, cold state (which divides head from heart, which demands order at the cost of passion) is deeply rooted in the nature of the Mexican peasants – especially in their customs and gestures. The occupants of the small, hilltop plaza must have light, and so makeshift globes are strung up over the trees; the remnants of churches still abound throughout Mexico; people still take their early evening walks, "women in one direction, men in the other," acting out their ritual of chaste separation; and in the police station, the peasants sit in archetypal postures with their hands between their knees.

External nature conspires against the state. Note that the plaza is like a small "island," surrounded by swamps and rivers and mountains, where unimpressed vultures (with "moron" faces) stare at the custodians of order, especially at the piglike jefe, whose clothes – his wide hat and flagrant cartridge belt – ironically and unintentionally resemble a bandit's (although he is a police officer).

Young Luis' father, in his resigned wit and in his ability to accept persons as they are, is "of the people." He is a vivid contrast to his wife, who wants to change human nature as much as the lieutenant does. Luis' father accepts the whiskey priest because at least the whiskey priest "carries on." And, then too, he feels that one cannot literally believe the Holy Books since *all* men are frail, even the saints. Besides, he reasons, if the whiskey priest had been reported and shot, his wife (Luis' mother) would now be reading about the whiskey priest to their son. Luis' father manifests the splendid ability of the Mexican peasants to penetrate myths – whether they are religious or antireligious myths.

Neither the inner world *nor* the outside world can be completely expunged from Mexico. One prisoner has hidden a sacred medal under his shirt, and the lieutenant fines him five pesos; Holy Books are smuggled in regularly from Mexico City. And the lieutenant hears a radio blaring out music which might be emanating from Mexico City, or even London or New York. Such remnants of the old society are as difficult to eradicate as the jefe's tooth is to extract. This tooth, incidentally, is finally treated – at the end of the novel, just as the priest-protagonist is being executed.

The picture of the murderer and bank robber, James Calver, stares out from the police station wall, as if in judgment, at the newly mounted (but old) photograph of the plump, complacent priest at a First Communion party of long ago. However, note that we never see the priest really "communicating" with his parishioners until he joins them in physical degradation. Ironically, the lieutenant spends his time hating what the priest *was,* not what he *is now.* Symbolically, as well as literally, the priest left Concepción years ago, although he retains traces of his morally smug past.

This idea of "purity" (which the lieutenant hates) first appeared in the initial chapter of the novel, when Tench was surprised by the expression on the priest's face when he (Tench) mentioned Lopez's former girl friend, now cohabiting with the Chief of Police. The priest's shocked facial expression was caused by his moral code and also because of the unexpected news that Lopez was the man whom he hoped would help him escape, the man who had helped other priests escape.

Before his "rebirth," later in the novel, the priest's pietism is a dramatic contrast to the pietism of Luis' mother, especially her senti-mentalized account of the boy martyr, young Juan. The story of young Juan is repugnantly *artificial* from start to finish, and it becomes the scroll upon which the *realistic* martyrdom of the unnamed, murdered priest will be engraved. Young Juan accepts even unjust rebuke with gratitude, and, in contrast, the priest thinks cynically of his bishop, who is safe from persecution. Young Juan will bravely cry out, "Long live Christ the King" at his execution, while the priest will be fear-ridden when his own death is imminent. The little play about the persecution of the early Christians, which young Juan acts in before his bishop, is in marked contrast to the priest's dramatic struggle; his own bishop, he is sure, does not even know he is alive. Juan's un-thinking morality is unquestionably destructive of true piety, and thus Greene awards him the part of Nero in the skit.

The theme of abandonment is taken up in this section, with the word itself used several times. Luis' father forgives the unnamed whiskey priest and Padre José for their lapses. All men are human, all abandoned in a seemingly God-forsaken Mexico.

Other key points in the chapter include the following: first, the lieutenant, in his desire to execute hostages until the last priest is found, reflects the totalitarian commonplace that the end justifies the means, *whatever* the means.

Second, Padre José is being "crucified" daily; his tedious existence with an overbearing wife is a daily martyrdom. (The sixty-two-year-old priest has been forced to marry because of state regulations.) As the chapter ends, he is called to bed by his shrewish wife, while a group of street children ridicule him. Padre José is a parody of St. Joseph, the patron saint of a happy family.

Third, the priest's drunken mistake of baptizing a boy "Brigitta," instead of "Pedro," probably (and symbolically) indicates his guilt — Pedro, or Peter, being the first head of the Church.

Finally, the drunken prisoner who cannot pay the five-peso fine and who is told to wash out the lavatories foreshadows the circum-stances of the priest's later arrest and imprisonment.

Chapter 3: *The River*

The scene changes: Captain Fellows, the director of the Central American Banana Company, is greeted by his wife, Trix, as he returns home from a business trip upriver. She informs him that a policeman (the lieutenant) is talking with their daughter, Coral, who arranged for the officer to sleep overnight on the veranda. Now, the officer is waiting to talk with Fellows.

Finding out nothing from Captain Fellows about the hunted "last priest," the lieutenant leaves the Fellowses, and Coral tells her shocked father that the priest whom the lieutenant is hunting is hiding in the barn. Coral saved the priest's life by refusing to give the lieutenant permission to search the premises. Later in the chapter, Coral brings the priest some food and a beer, and she promises to be his protector, always. In the barn, the priest explains to Coral that his attempted escape to Vera Cruz occurred a month ago. He wants to show the girl a card trick, but Coral doesn't have any cards. The priest then leaves the plantation and stumbles into a village, where, although exhausted, he is compelled to hear confessions because the people there have not been visited by a priest in five years.

In this chapter, then, we see that Captain Fellows is, like the priest, also "abandoned," but, in his placidity and moral obtuseness, he is *a happy man.* In contrast, the priest is *not* a happy man; he is sure that the bishop in Mexico City doesn't even know, or care, that he is alive. Unlike the priest, Fellows is irresponsible, and, despite his family's tenuous situation, he sings in his boat and savors the taste of his sandwich, a taste which is heightened by the open air. His eyes are blue and unreflecting, and his memory is porous.

Fellows is a Pilate-figure; he backs away from any human involvement. He warns Coral not to aid the priest since he fears the authorities, at whose sufferance he is living in Mexico. He speaks as Pilate might have done when deciding Christ's fate: "We've no business interfering in their politics." Fellows then pompously censures the priest's request for brandy.

With eyes like lakes at the top of a mountain, Captain Fellows is momentarily serene in his aloneness. He turns his problems away before they can affect him; to him, predatory alligators become mere trout in his song. He sings loudly to himself and, except for the sound of his motorboat, he is completely alone as he reminisces about his wartime experiences. He is unable to understand the subtleties of psychological fears, even though he was, apparently, a good soldier, especially when danger was clear-cut and visible. He constantly harkens back to a previous time of courage at zero-hour, humming songs vaguely remembered from the war-torn trenches of France. Fellows no longer has a guiding principle to his life, and he makes up his rules of conduct very much like he composes his disjointed lyrics – that is, to fit the occasion. He avoids specific problems: his wife's fear of death, fever, and the encroaching wilderness, and his daughter's beginning maturity, with its incipient sex drive.

Greene's attitude toward Fellows is clearly seen in the episode when the monkey jabbers at him as he sings; likewise, Fellows' command of a "banana company" helps to define his simian nature. Fellows operates on the basic level of animal survival; he lacks the complexity to be at one with the universe.

Mrs. Fellows is unmoved by her husband's fumbling efforts to reassure her; her life is a constant avoidance of words which suggest the family's dire condition. She is devoid of common sense and lives in constant terror and dissatisfaction.

Greene puns upon Mrs. Fellows' nickname, "Trix," just as he suggests that her husband is a symbol of false fellowship. When we first hear her name, we learn that she is playing a "trick" on her approaching mate, donning a mask of "frightened welcome." Later, the priest wants to demonstrate a card trick for Coral, who has been deceitfully impressed into responsibility by her neurotic parents – but Coral doesn't have a deck of cards.

Many characters in this novel trick both themselves and others in their attempts to implement false systems of value. Mrs. Fellows' self-deceit is seen in her fevers and in her complaints about the heat, both of which are physical objectifications of her suppressed emotions – that is, her inability to face life.

Coral, although she is only about thirteen, runs the household, and, when we learn of her death later in the novel, we see that the Fellowses are unable to exchange even the platitudes which once held them together. Before the judging gaze of their daughter's eyes here, the parents become "a boy you couldn't trust and a ghost you could almost puff away."

Coral's independence is evidenced in her assumption of responsibility during her father's absence, and in her seeing that the lieutenant (although she doesn't care for him) secures a place to sleep on the veranda. Greene calls attention to Coral's bravery in letting the priest remain in the barn during the night while the officer spends the night on the veranda of the house. In a matter-of-fact way, Coral informs her astonished father that she has hidden the priest and that she did not trust her panicky mother enough to share the secret with her.

Coral's emotions have not kept pace with her organizational abilities. She kisses her father perfunctorily, and she regards her assistance to the priest as an opportunity to learn geography and history. She glibly suggests to the priest that he "renounce his faith" merely because she has just learned the phrase while studying European history. When she pertly announces that she is an atheist and that she lost her faith at ten, she speaks very much like a developing thirteen-year-old girl, one who is emotionally very juvenile. And yet there is something of the compulsive fanatic about Coral; in that sense, she parallels the cold pragmatism of the lieutenant.

Coral attaches little meaning to her words. She is a child lost in a spiritual, physical, and emotional wilderness, where other children eat wormy dirt from the river bank. She mouths such expressions as "fugitive from justice" and prattles on about the Reform Bill, which 'extended voting rights in England, while she lives in a totalitarian environment.

Yet there is a basic, undeveloped kindness about Coral, for she does not shine the light in the priest's eyes as she enters the barn, as her father did. Greene cleverly uses Coral's innocence of theology to provide exposition. To Coral, the priest explains that he is not allowed to give himself up even if he wanted to. It is his duty *not* to be captured so that he can continue his ministry.

The lieutenant feels nothing but contempt for the Fellows family, hating them for the same reasons that he despises the clergy – their complacency and their love of ease. He knows restraint, however. He will not move an inch to greet the approaching Captain Fellows, and he properly hides his disgust by walking some distance away from Fellows before spitting.

Greene provides motivation for the lieutenant's actions. Captain Fellows complains that the police do not trust him, yet he previously told his wife that Coral should not have been left alone with the officer: "These fellows [an ironic word choice], you can't trust them." Greene explicitly compares the lieutenant to the priest: ". . . a little dark menacing question mark in the sun."

Animal imagery in the chapter is used to reinforce the hounded nature of the escaping priest. He evades the police only to become a servant to the faithful villagers, who have not seen a priest in five years. Allusions to animals also depict an inhuman society in which all emotions are reduced to a sub-human level.

Unpleasant images of animals (especially dogs) and vermin abound. A buzzard silhouetted against the sky taints Fellows' river excursion. Greene's description of Mrs. Fellows' "trick" of donning a mask of "frightened welcome" includes the information that the trick was not like that of suddenly sketching a dog, but, instead, of sketching a quick outline of a dog turned into a sausage. In addition, Coral would have "set the dogs" on the lieutenant had he tried to search the premises. And as Greene cites Coral's incredible awareness, he comments that in forty years, Coral's parents will be "as dead as last year's dog."

The priest also receives his share of animal imagery. Sucking his beer bottle in the barn, he resembles a cub being ministered to by his "mother," Coral. His breath is rancid, something like a rotting animal or like moldering debris left out in the sun. The priest's eating like an animal foreshadows his later fight with a starving dog over a scrap of meat left on a bone.

In the little village, the priest is compared to a bull in a ring, with the parishioners goading the tired clergyman. They want his services, but they fear the police. Even in the usable huts, rats move about at will, and one rat even "stares" at the priest as he tries to rest. With fine irony, as the priest weeps from exhaustion, Greene points out that the priest's host feels that the priest is crying over the sins of the old man's community; therefore, he urges his friends to confess lest they insult the priest, who is too exhausted already to hear great numbers of confessions.

The priest's use of the stable to hide from the questioning lieutenant and his use of the hut in the village suggest Christ's shelter at the time of his birth, and throughout *The Power and the Glory*, the priest makes several sporadic attempts at spiritual self-rejuvenation. Although he finds it difficult to help himself at this time, the priest's act of keeping the fire alive in the village represents his ability to keep the meager embers of the villagers' faith burning. When he blows on the fire, smoke fills the hut in this sacramental ceremony. Ironically,

Padre José was the last priest to visit the people, five years previously, as Greene continues to further compare the two clergymen.

The priest is also matched with Mrs. Fellows by Greene's use of the word "train." The priest clutches his attache case to him like a man awaiting a train that he must board, and Mrs. Fellows, dreaming of weddings, warns someone not to step on her train. For both people, a train is the means to an alluring but elusive future, one which neither will reach. When the trains *do* run in this novel, they head for ruined bridges and broken tracks, with Greene concluding that one cannot control the destiny of a loved one.

The characters in this chapter garner no symbolic illumination from the ever-present blanching sun. Their lives become maniacal attempts to ward off approaching death, and their efforts are continually thwarted by their prejudices. With death—emotionally and physically—all around him, Fellows can think only of a "dago secretary" and cite to Coral a tired distinction between social drinking and alcoholism.

Chapter 4: *The Bystanders*

In this chapter, structured like a multi-scene collage, Greene shows us: Mr. Tench, the dentist, waiting for a patient and beginning a letter to his estranged wife, Sylvia, and then hearing the bell of the *General Obregon*; the frail old ship has returned from Vera Cruz.

Meanwhile, Padre José, fearing that little Anita's relatives might boast if he were to say an "official" prayer over her body before it is placed in the ground, refuses to do so. In another part of town, Luis rejects the cloying piety of his deeply religious mother as she reads to him and his sisters. And in still another part of town, the thirteen-year-old Coral Fellows, assuming the responsibilities of her deficient parents, orders a load of bananas to be carried quickly to the quay for shipment on the *General Obregon*. In the cantina, the lieutenant learns that the Governor has given permission for him to shoot hostages so that the "last priest" can be taken before the rainy season sets in; neither the jefe nor the Governor, however, will put such orders in writing. Luis and some other boys admire the lieutenant's pistol, an act which will be in vivid contrast to what happens in the last chapter of this novel, when Luis, after the priest's execution, spits on the lieutenant's gun.

Clearly, each of the characters in this episode seeks to draw sustenance from the past, and in every instance the effort is doomed to futility. Tench writes to his wife merely to let *someone* know that he is still alive. Ironically, he relies upon time obliterating the memory of his handwriting from the mind of his dominating, interfering mother-in-law, Mrs. Marsdyke. As a dentist, he is used to pain; pain has little meaning anymore. He has ceased to feel, and like Padre José, he would rather feel homesickness than feel nothing at all.

In this context, note that Luis' father excuses his wife's devotion to the sentimentalized Holy Book because the tome represents all that is left of the feelings of childhood within the Mexican people. In contrast, young Coral Fellows has never had a child's past; she lost both her faith and her feelings of sentimentality and tenderness when she was ten. She has been "crucified" psychologically – and here, physiologically, as well, particularly in the scene when she wearily leans her aching shoulder blades against the scorching wall.

In the most dire straits, the characters think mainly of etiquette and social image. The family members of the dead little girl, Anita, we are inclined to believe, will want to boast that Padre José said a prayer at her grave. Anita's mother feels that Padre José should explain why her daughter died so young and caused so much inconvenience; Padre José feels a sense of pride at being addressed again as a priest, even though he is too timorous to conduct a brief religious ceremony. Likewise, the lieutenant fears that the gross, anticlerical, painted murals might damage the image of his progressive state: "He wanted to eliminate anything in the state at which a foreigner might have cause to sneer."

In this chapter, then, these characters, so concerned with *appearance,* are revealed to be thoroughly *selfish.* Tench, for example, realizes that his letter might prove embarrassing to his wife if she has married again, but he reasons that she need only tear it up. He never considers that the letter might be intercepted. Tench's selfishness, as with the selfishness of the others, is born of the deep and *hopeless emptiness* that has overwhelmed the Mexican state.

At times, spiritual emptiness finds its correlative in physical objects. A sign enjoins "Silence" as Padre José enters what was once the Garden of God; inside the larger tombs in the cemetery, the atmosphere resembles that of a kitchen in an *abandoned* house, perhaps one like that which the Fellowses are soon to leave behind. The coffin of Anita can be moved by a slight push of a shoe, for it seems to house nothing but *bones*. The 9:30 curfew helps create a sense of *sterility* when the resigned father of Luis stares out into the *dark* street, while beetles crawl on *broken wings* across the floor of his home. The lieutenant, thinking of his *vacant* universe, explains to Luis that he has never killed anyone with his gun—not yet, but the deadly weapon is a *copy* of an American pistol.

Empty words, empty dreams, and empty futures figure prominently in the chapter. The Tenches have exchanged letters only once since their little boy died. In addition, the death of Tench's child relates him to Fellows, who is soon to lose a daughter, and to the priest, whose daughter, we will discover, is *spiritually dead.* The letters which Coral receives from Private Tutorials, Ltd., are, at best, perfunctory and always six weeks late. The phony certificates which she gains from her studies are not even signed by Henry Beckley, the director, but are simply rubber-stamped.

Perhaps Luis' father best illustrates the emotional void of the Mexican people. Although he admits that he was not a good Catholic when the Church still flourished in Mexico, he truly misses the *ceremonies*— the music and the lights. Now there is nothing: "If we had a theatre, anything at all instead, we shouldn't feel so—left"—in other words, so *abandoned.* His attitude is contrasted with the futile hope of Anita's relatives. They were content to live with the *hopelessness* of burying the girl without proper religious obsequies, but with the appearance of Padre José and his rejection of their pleas, they experience an emotion even worse than before: despair.

Padre José is filled with despair, and he knows that he is committing a terrible sin by living in despair; he believes that he is so damned that God's mercy and grace cannot operate for him. Despair and presumption (the belief that God will save every man no matter what he has done) are the two sins which cannot be forgiven since they preclude a state of being contrite—that is, having a sincere, remorseful heart. Padre José is in the grip of despair when he acquiesces to the jeers of the mocking children and returns to his bed of sin. As Greene puts it, he commits the "unforgivable sin"—that is, succumbing to despair.

The characters' desolation of spirit is also seen in their complete lack of trust. Tench hesitates before opening his door to a patient. Anita's relatives beg Padre José to trust them—as their spokesman, an old man, repeats the word "trust" for emphasis. Padre José knows, however, that they *cannot* be trusted, that they will boast of the prayer, uttered by a priest, to the other townspeople.

Tench's crucible, with its gold alloy, resembles a blemished chalice. And with this in mind, note that Padre José washes his hands of responsibility in refusing to pray for Anita, as does Fellows in his lack of concern for the fugitive priest, who is himself corrupted.

The fat jefe and the thin lieutenant resemble a vaudeville team as they walk up the street. The comic futility of the Chief of Police is seen in the useless handkerchief which he wears knotted around his jaw in a wasted effort to stop the pain of his toothache. The exchange of the comedians is played out while the lieutenant attempts to force the jefe to commit himself about the killing of hostages.

Coral Fellows' characterization embraces many of Greene's motifs. Coral's premature sense of responsibility and her suffering at the hands of her inept parents are heightened by Greene's subtle description of her biochemical change. She has a slight headache, and her mother tells her that she thinks it will soon pass. Mrs. Fellows, however, avoiding issues as usual, doesn't explain the cause of the discomfort. When Coral asks about the Virgin Birth, her mother reacts like many parents who believe that references even to non-sex are *verboten*. Coral wonders why she feels so tired early in the day, and in a brilliant Christocentric symbol, which suggests that Coral is sacrificed to her parents' ignorance as well as to her blossoming body, Greene has Coral lean against the wall until her shoulders are scorched. Greene splendidly captures Coral's confusion as she experiences menstrual cramps for the first time. Like a child, Coral reasons that her pain is not caused by worms and then intuits that her body, in some near-miraculous way, has readied itself for these as-yet-not-understood changes. Greene is at his best in describing the wondrous moments of Coral's beginning womanhood, which is soon to be cut short by death.

Paralleling references to Coral's emotionally stunted youth are Greene's allusions to the delightfully pert aspects of a girl who could have offered a great deal to the world. Coral reminds her forgetful mother what day it is, and she also finds out on her own that her father has not gotten the produce ready for the boat. Accepting her responsibilities, she crisply orders the Indian worker to quicken his pace; then, when the job nears completion, Coral questions the workers twice to make sure that each batch of bananas has been accounted for. Hard-fact reality fills Coral Fellows' world.

In contrast, the falsity of the story of young Juan is diametrically opposed to the reality of Coral's fate – and to the fate of the fugitive priest. In a traditional and saccharin manner, Juan's family "mourns" the loss of young Juan, for he has decided to devote his life to God and to forsake family and the secular world. Ordained as a priest, Juan distributes the Holy Eucharist to his family, as Greene implies the dramatic discrepancy between a hard-won *human communication* and the *formalized communion service* in the Holy Book of Luis' mother.

In addition, *un*like the indulgent, alcoholic priest, young Juan spends his days mortifying (not satisfying) *his* flesh; that is, he denies himself even small physical comforts in return for spiritual rewards. In contrast, Greene's more human anti-hero, this "last priest," is so *un*disciplined that he cannot stop himself from begging brandy and from robbing a dying dog of a bone. But Juan subjects himself to utter mortification and physical deprivations which require the permission of a priest in Confession, and Juan has followed the appropriate forms. In all of this syrupy excess, Greene is saying that the Gospel according to John or, in this case, Juan, is *not* to be taken very seriously. In fact, the story of young Juan brings about the *opposite* of its intention. Luis, after listening to his mother's fervid recounting of the saintly lad's doings, gazes with rapt devotion at the lieutenant's pistol, an instrument of death. And finally, the play that young Juan will act in is set in the catacombs, ironically foreshadowing the resurrection of the hunted priest in prison.

Once again, this chapter reveals Greene's ability to tie a novel together by parallels and by a multitude of deftly connected scenes. The villagers who hound Padre José are like those villagers who would not let the priest sleep in the previous chapter. And here, as Coral Fellows enters the barn and finds crosses chalked on the wall, the action jumps ahead four days to the cantina where the jefe is chalking his billiard cue and is interrupted by the lieutenant. In his use of ironic juxtaposition, which is so much more important than mere chronology, Greene is suggesting that all things, both great and small, must be measured completely against the fullness of humanity.

Taking into consideration the many viewpoints of the characters in this chapter, the inked-in halo above the priest's picture on the prison wall suggests that he is closer to sainthood *now* than he was at Concepción, although he is the last one to realize this.

PART TWO

Chapter 1

A few weeks after his life has been saved by Coral Fellows, the priest, desperately trying to evade the soldiers, arrives in a tiny village. Maria, the mother of his child, Brigitta, who is now about six years old, lives here. The villagers ask the priest to say Mass for them, but they also urge him to leave very soon because a hostage named Pedro Montez, from Concepción, was shot by the police after wine (used in Mass) was found in the village.

The priest performs Mass, hurrying the service as the soldiers arrive. He barely avoids capture because his daughter identifies him first as "father" – then, as *her* father. Miguel, a young villager, is taken hostage because no one will betray the priest's presence, and later, Maria disposes of the priest's wine supply lest it be found by the authorities.

The second half of the chapter is linked to the first section because the priest must journey to a larger settlement in order to find a new supply of wine. There, he meets a mestizo, or half-caste, the "Judas figure" of the novel. The man insists on accompanying the priest to Carmen, the priest's birthplace. Unable to rid himself of the ill and persistently questioning half-caste, the priest finally admits that yes, he *is* a priest. But because of this confession, the priest is now unable to enter Carmen, for he knows that the mestizo will report him and collect the reward. Thus, at a fork in the road, two hours from the village, the priest sends the ill and feverish half-caste forward, help-lessly ill astride a mule, into Carmen. The half-caste, deprived of his seven-hundred-peso reward, weakly shouts back to the priest that he will *not* forget his face.

Because of this chapter's length, Greene wisely divides it into two narrative parts. Note, in this respect, that the priest is turned away from Maria's village at the end of the first part, and, at the conclusion of the second part, the priest is unable to enter Carmen because of the mestizo; he has to turn away, like Moses, who was almost at the destination where he hoped he would find peace.

Of interest also is the fact that the priest's estrangement (even with Maria and his daughter, he is merely a prisoner among prisoners) and, later in the chapter, his incipient charity toward the half-caste are *both* delineated by biblical allusions. Maria easily becomes Mary, the sister of Martha who once ministered to Christ. In addition, the cock crows three times during the chapter, suggesting Peter's betrayal of Christ, and, here, the "betrayal" of the murdered *Pedro* (Peter) Montez, and later, the half-caste's future betrayal of the priest. The "weight" at the back of the priest's tongue during his sermon correlates with the unworthiness he feels at receiving the Holy Eucharist while in the state of mortal sin.

The half-caste's two teeth, as well as his plump, yellow toe, which slithers forward like a forest animal's, place him squarely in Satan's camp, and the priest sees him as a mock Judas figure, like the one hanged during Holy Week ceremonies at his old parish. But, like the Good Samaritan, the priest lets his enemy use his mule as he himself walks Christ-like, with bleeding feet. Symbolically, the mule becomes the donkey which Christ rode into Jerusalem, and finally, the expression "watch and pray" in the flashback to Concepción suggests that the priest is now undergoing his Gethsemane.

The relationship of the priest to his daughter parallels the relationships of other adults to other children in the novel, all defining the *dual nature* of the priest's role as a spiritual parent and as a physical parent. Like Coral Fellows, Brigitta, the priest's "old-young" child, has had no typical "childhood." She is seemingly mature before her time, and she also seems to have Coral's godless bent. Brigitta laughs at her father much like the children ridicule Padre José, and she refuses to say her catechism, just as Luis will not listen to his mother read from the Holy Book. Like Luis, too, she reaches up to the lieutenant when he is on horseback. And also, like the dead Anita, she has been sickly from birth. In addition, the priest wants to show his daughter the card trick that he was previously unable to demonstrate to Coral. Again, symbolically, there are no cards.

Most significantly, both the priest *and* the lieutenant feel that *children are more important than anything else in the state,* and the use of the expression "my children" by Padre José and the escaping priest recalls similar sentiments of the lieutenant, who wants to obliterate the privations of his youth by reconstructing a new social order, especially for the children.

During his stay with Maria, the priest is exposed to all the ingredients of a "valid" family life, but he is unable to grasp them. He cannot "communicate" with Maria even though she provides him with bread and wine, hides him in bed when the soldiers approach, and has him chew an onion to cover the smell of wine on his breath.

Their lack of ultimate union is symbolized by the interrupted Mass which the priest says. Because of the approaching troops, he finishes the Consecration, but is unable to distribute Communion. In his lonely world, the priest, by theological mandate, consumes the Host himself rather than have it found and be desecrated by the police.

With justification, the priest reasons that Maria would have made a good wife, that he could be living with her in safety, were it not for his pride. Clearly, he trusts Maria completely, and although he knows she has reason to hate him (since she was only a sex partner for him), he goes to the village convinced that she will not betray him. Maria is a full woman – practical, informal, and even a bit proud that a priest once made love to her. She bridges the years easily, and like a wife, she complains of the priest's meager clothing, which makes him look so common. She would have repaired his former dark garb and hidden it. With her practical suggestion that the priest join her in bed to hide from the police, Maria is an excellent contrast to both Mrs. Fellows and to the slovenly, self-centered wife of Padre José.

Many of the priest's difficulties come from a formalistic theology and a tender conscience. Thinking of the Archangel Michael driving Satan from Heaven, he feels damned, a mortal sinner distributing the Eucharist. He feels guilty about his emotions for Brigitta, his child, conceived by serious sins. Constantly flickering through the priest's mind is the thought that by continuing his ministry in Mexico, he is violating a prime edict of the Church: a man is responsible for saving his *own* soul, first of all.

The priest's Jansenistic conscience is seen in his fear that returning to the place of his sin *might* be wrong; but he assuages his scrupulosity by considering the visit, the first one in six years, to be his *duty*. He worries, as well, about not using an altar stone during Mass, but he reasons that he is far from Church authority. He wishes to call the villagers "my children," but he concludes that only the childless man has the right to do so. The priest's ministry is objectified by the *chipped cup* which he uses for the Sacrament in place of his lost chalice.

Such lachrymose sentiments, however, are laced through with flashes of the priest's remaining sturdiness and integrity. He authoritatively reminds the peasants that his presence in the village is neither his businesss nor theirs – only God's. He remains in the forbidden country because of his stark thought of God's absence from so vast an area of land; without God, the country would be the empty universe of the lieutenant. Accordingly, the priest sublimates his deprivations in his sermon when he sincerely preaches that pain and joy are inextricable and that only by accepting pain can one gain Heaven, the end of all suffering.

The priest's *rebirth* begins with his realization that his attempts to be the only clergyman in good standing left in Mexico might have proceeded partly from pride, that the humble Padre José could well be the better priest. He begins to realize also that Christ died *even for the downtrodden half-caste*. From the priest's despair comes a human love, which is seen in his dire concern for his daughter, although here the priest still struggles between two types of fatherhood – spiritual and physical fatherhood.

The priest's previous exchange of clothing with the peasant reflects his now-growing humility, as does his telling the mestizo that the scrap of paper, clinched in his fist, and remaining from his days at Concepción, is a list of seeds. The *seeds of his ministry* only now have begun to bear fruit.

The beginning of the priest's rebirth is seen most clearly in his renewed love and respect for the impoverished congregation. The villagers bear pain and mortification voluntarily, whereas his pain and mortification have been forced upon him. Now he can begin to understand their ordeal, for he is no longer the aloof clergyman that he was in Concepción. Now he resembles the two men who kneel with arms outstretched in the form of the Cross during the Consecration, offering up their pain to God in expiation of their sins.

The redemption is starting just in time for the priest to be saved theologically. For example, the prayers which he says when he fears being shot by the lieutenant do not constitute "perfect contrition" – that is, sorrow for sin which proceeds solely from a love of God. Salvation through "imperfect contrition" (fear of Hell) demands that a priest hear the penitent's confession. Theologically, if the priest were shot and killed at this time, he would be doomed.

In his dilemmas, the priest differs utterly from the glib clergyman who ran up debts in Concepción, told insipid and inappropriate jokes to the solemn women of the parish, and spun pietistic tales much like the sugared stories of Luis' mother. Greene allows the priest to remember his recital concerning the eleven-year-old girl who died con-

tented, from consumption, because Greene is implying that young
Juan might well have become such a pompous, unchallenged, and
unchallenging priest.

Maria acts as a realistic corrective to the phony religiosity of Luis'
mother when she points out that the martyrdom of a whiskey priest
would be a scandal. And, too, the priest adds reality to the novel when
he realizes that his death and the death of the hostages might be occasioned by mere religious superstition. In fact, superstition becomes
a major theme in the overall book, a theme that is seen later in the
Indian mother's burial rites for her three-year-old child.

One last point about this chapter: Greene reinforces the priest's
sinful act of love by including several references to the color scarlet
in the section: a turkey's pink membrane, riding boots fringed with
scarlet, and a snake hissing through the grass "like a match flame."
Also, the smuggled book has a direct bearing on the priest's adultery:
A Husband for a Night.

Chapter 2

The events of this section take place a few months after the priest's
attempt to flee to Vera Cruz. In this capital city of a Mexican province,
the priest, dressed in a drill uniform, meets a beggar who promises
to secure wine for him. And, sure enough, before long, the priest,
and the cousin of the Governor, the jefe, and a beggar are in a hotel
room, all drinking. They drink all of the grape wine (needed by the
priest if he is to say Mass), and finally, the priest is left with only
a largely depleted bottle of brandy (not suitable for the Consecration—
when the wine is changed into the blood of Christ).

Afterward, the priest is pursued by Red Shirts when his bottle
of brandy chinks against the wall of the cantina which he has entered
to escape the rain. Followed a spirited chase, during which Padre José
refuses to hide him, the priest is thrown into a dank, dark prison cell,
charged with the crime of possessing contraband liquor. In addition,
we know that the mestizo, who says that he can identify the priest,
is being held by the police for that very purpose.

Clearly, many themes and motifs enunciated earlier in the novel
reappear in this chapter, as well as in the crucial chapter that follows,
which in many ways is the center of *The Power and the Glory*. Here,
in Chapter 2, there are the same empty ceremonies that we will
discover in Chapter 3, as well as similar animal imagery, recurrences

of fraudulent social amenities, and a play upon the word "trust," all of which help to unify the chapters, and in addition, there is much Christocentric symbolism. This particular chapter hinges upon a bizarre perversion of a Communion service—wine shared in a bleak bedroom, while the wrong people consume the wine meant for Mass—and finally, the priest is left with only brandy, totally unusable for the celebration of Mass. Meanwhile, outside, a violent storm intensifies the priest's inner terror and shame.

The chapter begins with the mechanical promenading of the young men and women of the village, all silent, the sexes moving in separate directions. Greene explicitly characterizes the sterile practice: "It was like a religious ceremony which had lost all meaning, but at which they still wore their best clothes." Only the old women who impulsively join in the march vivify the empty, meaningless procession, and Greene suggests that only they (perhaps) retain some of the occasional good humor which was common in the days before the Red Shirts. Outside the ring of marchers, the old grandmothers rock idly back and forth in their chairs, surrounded by relics of a better past, the family photographs. Greene muses upon the irony of such activities forming the nucleus of a Mexican state's capital city.

The taxicab drivers mirror the vacuity of their country as they wait for fares that never materialize, and the hotel where the abortive Eucharistic feast is to take place boasts the names of only three guests for its twenty rooms. Sheltered from a fierce storm, both meteorological and political, the principal characters repeat hollow theological expressions which have lost the core of their meaning. Later, when a Red Shirt misses his billiard shot, he automatically responds with an outcry to the Virgin Mary. Significantly, this exclamation (a sort of perverted prayer, as it were) is *accidentally* caused by the priest, who bumps the Red Shirt's arm as he is about to shoot.

Each character here plays a social role opposite to his real nature, and Greene suggests that the resultant mask is indigenous to a state which has lost *all contact* with theological truth. The drill suit worn by the priest is delightfully ambiguous; this is Greene's comment upon the authoritarian nature of the Church, as well as his suggestions that the ideals of the priest and the lieutenant are in many ways interchangeable.

The priest and the other men in the hotel room observe all the artificial "rules" of social drinking etiquette. At the instigation of the beggar, the priest offers his fiercely prized wine to the influential cousin of the Governor – because in a topsy-turvy state, the *least worthy* people become the most powerful people. From the start, then, the bottle of wine that was destined to be used for Mass, is doomed, and the custodians of the nation consume it just as they have consumed the Church.

The Governor's cousin quickly moves from his uneasy role of pseudo-official to his real nature as a sloppy extrovert and drinking companion. Still, however, he officiously warns the priest that Vera Cruz ("true cross") brandy is contraband, and then he dismisses unheard the priest's protest that he is only interested in buying wine. Playing his authoritarian role to the full, he cautions the priest that he could have him arrested, and the priest is forced into an abject and feeble defense of his desire to buy some wine.

The ill-fitting clothes of the Governor's cousin correlate with his awkward handling of power, and as soon as the priest agrees to pay extra for wine, the man abruptly drops his authoritative mask and wheedles several libations from the fugitive. With his pasty face and tight suit, the Governor's cousin, except for his bulging weapon, resembles a servant or waiter more than he does a man of political consequence.

The priest is victimized by hollow social forms and the awkward changes in personality that accompany them. He is tense and subservient to the Governor's cousin and is afraid to deny his request that toasts be made with the precious wine. And later, note that the priest's capture is brought about by bored Red Shirts who are trying more to have fun at the priest's expense than to enforce prohibition. After they catch him, they treat him with familiar jocularity. They resemble children playing a game of hide-and-seek; in fact, the Red Shirt whose billiard shot the priest spoils is barely past adolescence.

This juvenile sociability continues as the priest is marched to jail, with the Red Shirts telling jokes and mildly joshing the priest about his effort to escape. Even the jailer pats him reassuringly as he slams the cell door behind him.

Physical deterioration and mechanical ineptitude accompany this political breakdown in social norms, with Greene suggesting that the mechanism of the Marxist state is indeed creaky. The dynamo in this scene, in the only hotel in town, operates in fits and starts, and it churns throughout the wine drinking, suggesting the frustrated energies of the state. Note that the beggar and the priest enter the hotel, and the "light" almost goes out; then it flickers on again and mirrors the priest's *physical and spiritual* state – his *slight* hope that he *might* say Mass again, *if* he can obtain some wine.

Other small details in the chapter add to the total picture of the ineffectual nation. With its single iron bed, the room foreshadows the priest's later entrance into the abandoned Fellows' home. Gaps in the mosquito netting allow beetles to enter the room, and the stairs leading to the first floor are covered with the hard-shelled black insects. The shoes of the Governor's cousin squeak on the tiles, and he draws the forbidden liquor from a large tear in the mattress. Above the hotel, the sharp, nail-like rain provides no respite from the heat, for the city is as suffocating after the cloudburst as it was before.

Not surprisingly, trust is utterly lacking among the principals in this chapter. They constantly lie to each other, and their machinations form a microcosm of the nation. The beggar earns his commission by telling the priest that the Governor's cousin will sell liquor only to someone whom he "trusts" – that is, the beggar. He worked for the Governor's cousin once and apparently knows the location of the skeletons in his closet. The beggar explains that the cousin gets his liquor free from customs; yet shortly afterward, the official tells the priest that he comes by the liquor legally and must pay for it. He cites a humanitarian motive behind his wine collecting and states that he charges *only* what he himself paid for it. The Governor's cousin is shocked to learn that the priest gave fifteen pesos to the beggar for the brandy.

The jefe is judged a bland person, but clearly he cannot be trusted at billiards, and note that he insists upon calling the illegal wine "beer" throughout the episode. One is reminded of his refusal to assume responsibility in the shooting of hostages. Also, he knowingly refers to the "dregs" at the bottom of the "beer" bottle, and later, he jokingly pretends that he is drinking sidral.

At the jail, the lies continue. The Red Shirt and the policeman argue about whether or not the lieutenant should be disturbed since the fine is only five pesos. The Red Shirt wonders, however, who will get the money, and in one of the infrequent humorous moments in the novel, the priest announces that no one will, since he has only twenty-five centavos.

In a world of such hypocrisy and deceit, any symbolic Eucharistic service must be hollow, and in this chapter the theology of the "cele-brants" is as sterile as that of the lieutenant. The only true celebrant, the fleeing priest, never gets the opportunity to consume the wine (intended for Mass), for Greene hinges this important episode on a fine point of Church law: wine used at a Mass *must* consist of no more than fifteen percent alcohol; brandy, of course, is high in alcoholic content. Also, Mass wine *must* be made from grapes, and thus, the priest quickly rejects the quince product. He needs either a French or a California wine. Greene describes the priest's need for the ceremonial wine in terms of an alcoholic's craving when the priest tells the mestizo that he would give almost all that he has to slake his thirst. In doing God's work, the priest draws upon very personal knowledge of alcoholic addiction.

The events surrounding the consumption of the wine, then, take on sacramental importance, with four men attending the celebration— the priest, the Governor's cousin, the beggar, and later, the Chief of Police. The priest's pretense of wanting to take the remainder of the wine back to his mother hints of his wish to reestablish ties with the Mother Church of Rome. In this context, the beggar's avowal that he too has a mother points to the residual, even though unconscious, theological instincts in the Mexican people.

The wine is explicitly connected to the Eucharist when the jefe relates his earliest memory, his First Communion. But so little atten-tion is paid to his comment that a joke is made concerning the impos-sibility of two parents standing "around" the corpulent officer. The jefe's remark, however, does tie things together, for he announces that it was his duty to see that the priest who administered the sacrament to him is shot to death. Also, the priest's constantly recurring memory throughout the novel is that of a First Communion celebration. The bond between the dead priest and the living priest, then, is strong, and at the end of *The Power and the Glory*, a new priest arrives to take up the duties of the protagonist, who has been executed.

Other, more subtle references to Christian practices and traditions reinforce the idea of wine as the prime symbol of a missing ingredient in an unconsummated Communion. The rain suggests the Crucifixion, and it falls as if "it were driving nails into a coffin lid" while the priest's doom is being worked out through his transient companions' thirst for the precious wine. Padre José, to whom the priest turns for help as he flees the Red Shirts, is a mockery of a priest, with his billowing white nightshirt resembling the chasuble and alb worn by a priest at Mass. The alb, as the name implies, is the long "white" covering which reaches to the celebrant's heels. The lamp which Padre José holds is a symbolic reminder of a candle, perhaps of the type that the fallen clergyman might have used at a former church ceremony.

The pursued priest actually "confesses" to Padre José, even though the act lacks the needed formal dispositions. The protagonist tells Padre José of his past pride and swears that he always knew that Padre José was the better man. Here, the priest's humanistic confession, especially the revelation of his self-awareness, is more meaningful in Greene's eyes than a formal disavowal of sin, although the Church insists upon the latter as being necessary for salvation. Just before the young, disdainful Red Shirt arrives, Padre José's wife, like a jaded guardian angel, draws her husband away from any involvement.

The priest's flight from the Red Shirts is his Gethsemane, his suffering in the Garden of Olives, although in this novel his pain—in contrast to Christ's—is heightened because death, for the priest, is several times postponed. The priest is crucified by alcohol, as well as by the state, and his drunken sweat symbolically resembles Christ's "sweat" of blood. Also, the ridicule directed at the priest by the guards, although it is largely harmless, reflects Christ's demeaning treatment by the Roman soldiers after his capture following the Holy Thursday Last Supper. The priest, like Christ, allows himself to be led away by the authorities, but as a "bowed servile figure," he can think only of *his own preservation.*

Greene makes the parallels to Holy Week traditions explicit in three ways. The servant's large key resembles an object from a morality play, a Medieval dramatization of Christian allegory; the priest asks for water in his cell, but he is refused—just as Christ was given vinegar mixed with gall by His executioners; and, most important, the lieutenant slaps a sentry upon the ear, an act strongly suggesting St. Peter's cutting off a soldier's ear in an act directed against one who dared to lay hands on the Savior.

The priest's martyrdom, like that of the peasants, is carried out on the excruciating rack of the day-in and day-out despair that infects the whole of Greene's Mexico. Everyone is affected by the boredom and filth of the capital city, and most of them are reduced to a near-animal level of emotional responsiveness. The priest is clearly compared to a rat caught in a maze as he is chased by the predatory Red

Shirts through darkened, winding streets which are hidden from the moonlight. The professional hunters, the police, join in the search and add methodology to the chase, resembling natives beating the bushes for a wild animal.

The matter of the search for the priest becoming an "animal hunt" is cleverly foreshadowed in the chapter. Earlier, as the priest spoke with the beggar, the thunder was said to sound like the noise of a Sunday bullfight from across town, and the image suggests the comparison of the priest to a wounded bull, a parallel drawn earlier in the novel. As the police are leading the mestizo toward jail at the start of the chapter, the beggar assures the priest – that is, the stranger in the drill uniform – that the two of them need not be afraid: the police are looking for "bigger game." In the hotel room, the Chief of Police assures the group that the priest will soon be caught, for the mestizo has been set on his tracks like a bloodhound.

The bestial nature of this jungle world is seen in the fetid surroundings of the residents and in their coarse actions. Greene cites the "sour green smell" that rises from the river, and the image is effective, even though smells do not ordinarily have color. The Governor's cousin spits on the tiles of the hotel room to authenticate his pretended annoyance at being asked to find wine for the stranger. In addition, Padre José spits at the priest, refusing to hear his confession, but so impotent is this married priest that his spittle falls short of its target. The men sleeping in hammocks in the courtyard are said to be like chickens tied up in nets, and note, too, that the jaw of one man hangs over the side of a hammock like a piece of meat on a butcher's counter. All of this description sets the stage for the Purgatory-like setting of the following chapter.

The priest's existence in the midst of such sordidness is lonely indeed; he is stripped of all the amenities that once characterized his office. He completes his "confession" to Padre José by dropping the ball of paper saved from his Concepción days at the base of Padre José's wall. His act denotes his fear of being defeated by the Red Shirts, and it also symbolizes his easing off the officiousness and pomposity of his past life. In other words, he wishes to meet his Maker naked, as it were.

The priest faces what he anticipates to be his death, unfettered by material goods or money, or even decent clothing. Later, his official nature emerges again briefly at the Lehrs' home, but then he is able to recognize his backsliding and return to his true mission. Now he is dressed in a shabby drill uniform, watching the lights, which have been awkwardly strung together, and the promenaders. He even looks like an alcoholic, having several cuts on his face as evidence of a desire to shave too closely with a trembling hand. Again, Greene sees the priest as a lapsed businessman, this time one without an attache case – indeed, as a businessman who is bankrupt.

Ironically, the fact of his alcoholism allows the priest to be accepted by the beggar. Likewise, the Governor's cousin will trust him because he looks like a drinker. Then, too, he is able to keep a secret, and Greene may have in mind the priest's many years of keeping the secrecy of the confessional. The beggar is sure that he will return to the Governor's cousin for more liquor in the future.

The priest is not yet fully purged; perhaps, we must assume, he never will be. Thus, we are somewhat prepared for his being somewhat inebriated later, when he is executed at the end of the novel. In fact, he is shaking so terribly with fear and alcoholic tremors that he has to be led to the place of execution because his legs will not support him. And in this chapter, Greene emphasizes that the priest's addiction to brandy betrays him into weeping in front of the group, and later, into being captured. The clinking sound of the nearly empty bottle alerts the Red Shirts to the forbidden liquor.

In many ways, the beggar resembles the half-caste mestizo, for Greene implies that both men are products of a type of life that the priest ignored during his ministry – when he catered to the more solvent Mexican Catholics. The priest does not know how to relate to the beggar, and his temporizing efforts succeed merely in annoying his companion. As with the half-caste, the priest treats the underling's immediate and dire concerns as if they were elements in a theological disputation. He states that a starving man has the right to save himself. The priest's abstractions merely lead the beggar to see him as cold and unfeeling.

Throughout the chapter, the beggar's ways are those of the half-caste, the other minor "demon" who plagues the protagonist and eventually helps to bring about his final capture. The beggar's attitude alternates between confidential whispers and threats, and the slapping of his feet on the pavement recalls the barefoot walk of the half-caste through the forest. In addition, his attempts at further confidentiality add merely a darker, even more artificial tone to his relationship with the priest. His closeness remains merely physical, in spite of his touching the priest's leg with his own and placing his hand on the priest's sleeve, much as a former parishioner might have done in asking a blessing. The description of the two men as possible brothers is darkly ironic.

In conclusion, the priest's meeting with the beggar is as accidental as was his encounter with the mestizo in the last chapter. And although the priest's eyes meet the latter's, there is no spiritual recognition. The column of police continues its march with the informer, whose two fang-like, Satanic teeth jut out over his lip. For the moment, the half-caste is more interested in being cared for by the authorities than he is in immediately betraying his chance acquaintance.

Finally, the chapter reveals once again Greene's skilled use of exposition. The jefe tells the group in the room that the arrival of the rains is bad luck for his men; his words follow in response to the symbolic lightning and thunder outside the hotel. We learn too that news of the hidden priest surfaced only a few months before and that it is the Governor, not the jefe, who is obsessed with his capture. Also, in the midst of the wine drinking, it is the priest, the man in the drill uniform, who takes this opportunity to ask about the number of hostages shot. The answer, "three or four perhaps," enlightens the reader as well as the quietly suffering clergyman.

Chapter 3

The priest spends the night in prison while a couple make love in a filthy corner of the dark cell. He talks with an old man whose daughter has been taken from him by the Church priests because she is illegitimate, and he also talks with a proud, self-righteous woman whose haughty morality he tries unsuccessfully to change.

Next morning, unable to pay his fine, the priest is forced to empty the pails of human excrement and then wash out six prison cells. In one of these, he encounters the half-caste mestizo, who says that he will not turn in the priest – at this time – because he will get a larger reward if he identifies the priest *outside* of the jail setting. The priest also comes upon the hostage Miguel, who has been badly beaten. Finally, the lieutenant ends the episode by taking pity upon the priest and giving him a five-peso coin because he thinks that the apparently aging protagonist will not be able to work very much longer.

The priest's night in prison and his captivity form a microcosm of the entire novel, and thus Greene pulls together many motifs, symbols, and threads of narrative found throughout *The Power and the Glory*. The pious woman, whose complacency the priest is unable to shake, combines traits of Luis' mother with characteristics of the hypocritically self-righteous women whom the young priest catered to in Concepción. She contrasts sharply with the love-making couple; because of her pietism and her reliance upon the "forms" of religion, she cannot share the other woman's sense of abandonment to another human being. To the priest, the pious woman typifies those who garner their holy pictures and, like Luis' mother, take pride in the "good books" in their homes. She is also the type of person described at the start of the preceding chapter, rocking unproductively in her chair amidst family photographs, and she is graphically defined by her teeth: unlike those of the other principals in the work, hers are strong — but they resemble tombstones.

The woman is hard and sterile and comes to symbolize the death of the spirit, especially when she walks off with her sister, both of them wearing black shawls. The pious woman's censure of Catarina's father shocks the priest, whose daughter is *also* illegitimate *and* permanently estranged from him. When the old woman insists that the priests were right in taking the old man's daughter from him, the fugitive priest, after only a moment's delay, affirms that *he is a priest*. Probably the woman's glib enunciation that priests are *always* correct, even in matters of the emotions, has forced his hand.

After the priest has confessed his identity to the group, the pious woman tries to convert him, seeing him as a possible "good thief." Her actions, ludicrous and supercilious as they are, foreshadow the priest's later attempts to save Calver from Hell as he lies dying. Tireless in her moral sterility, the woman pleads that a drinking problem can be forgiven, but that she cannot forgive his sympathy for the "animals" who are making love amidst the dark stench of the prison. And when the priest frankly states that at the moment he would rather have a drink than God, the furious woman agrees that he is indeed an evil priest. She will write a complaint to the bishop!

The chapter is tied to the rest of the novel in many other, more diverse ways. Note the muffled noise of voices in prison; they resemble the sounds of an electric belt on a small machine, and one is reminded of the chugging dynamo in the hotel, in the previous chapter.

The act of love, consummated in the sour darkness, among the other prisoners, is very much like the passion of the priest for Maria, carried out in the midst of the priest's drinking and loneliness. Also, when the priest expresses his fear of pain at death, he is told that a toothache is much worse. One is reminded of Tench and the jefe. And just as the priest is thinking of himself as a martyr, he giggles and remembers Maria's injunction that it would be wrong to bring ridicule upon the Church. Here, the priest's "sermon" in prison resembles his words to the villagers at Mass earlier in the novel. Now, however, the priest's strident moralizing is tempered by compassion; here, *he* is the one who is confessing.

Other, smaller similarities relate this chapter to the entirety of the novel. The pious woman's addiction to holy pictures is like the priest's need, now overcome, for the wad of paper that once reminded him of Concepción. His suggestion that the loud woman in prison say an Act of Contrition (since there is no privacy in the cell for Confession) is lame, ignoring the priest's certainty that such an act, for him at least, is impossible. Also, the priest again realizes that he cannot say Mass, and thus, the chapter is related immediately to the preceding one: the wine has trickled away, down the throats of the jefe and the Governor's cousin. And whereas the priest was not able to communicate meaningfully with the other men during the drinking episode, here in prison, he *is* able to communicate—here, where faces cannot be seen. This last detail is significant because the priest is used to speaking to penitents in a dark confessional. Also, the notion of writing to the bishop blends with a number of other useless messages in the novel.

In addition, Greene uses the recurrent images of a door and an abandoned house to describe the priest's thoughts about his uniform, which he will no longer need—just as a voice in the yard calls out his assumed name, "Montez." The image of a door figures prominently in the dream which the priest has as he dozes off for a few seconds during the pious woman's lament for her missed vocation. The dream manifests much of the guilt which lies just below the priest's consciousness—guilt associated with his need for a password to attain salvation, probably a reference to his inability to formulate an act of Perfect Contrition; guilt associated with Coral; guilt associated with California grape wine; guilt when he claimed to be a "quack" (doctor) in the opening scenes of the novel; and finally, the dream manifests the priest's guilt connected with his inability to affect his daughter's future, to save her from spiritual death and/or middle-aged complacency.

Christocentric imagery, as well, holds the chapter together, as the priest's actions are compared to Christ's. The chapter combines elements of the Last Supper on Holy Thursday with Christ's descent into Hell (or Limbo) after His death, following the Crucifixion on Good Friday. On Holy Thursday, Christ washed the feet of the Apostles; here, the priest empties full buckets of human waste materials into a latrine. When Christ descended into Hell after his death, he freed the worthy souls, who had been waiting since the start of the human race for Christian redemption. In Greene's uncompromising view of the priest's ministry, the effects of the priest's words will never be known.

Greene's priest comes to the cell as empty and as forsaken as Christ must have been on the evening of His betrayal. He has nothing— no cigarettes, or water, or food, or money; and he must give a negative response to all the requests of the inmates. Greene invests the passage with a biblical tone by stating that one could count to forty between the lightning flash and the roll of thunder and, shortly afterward, one can conclude that the cell could not be more than twelve feet deep. The fact that the priest is halfway between the mountains and the sea confirms his desolation; and in the cell, he does not have enough room to move an inch, as he awaits the dawn with cramped legs. Reinforcing the Christocentric symbolism is the pious woman's explanation of the old man's arrest: he was found in possession of a crucifix. The object suggests the old man's crucifixion by ecclesiastical authorities, in the same way that Catarina was taken away.

In addition, the priest's feet, with their cramped soles, hurt him very much, and after the pain, they become numb. The priest shares traits of the "good thief," and the pious woman's allusion to this tradition is more relevant than she imagines. The priest undergoes the pain in his shoulders, for example, as the "good thief" did and as Christ did—for a charitable reason. He wants to give the old man room enough to sleep, and then too, he is sorry for whatever harm priests like himself did to the father when they took his daughter away from him.

The priest is "stripped of his garments" toward the end of his stay in the cell when he realizes that the drill suit has been ruined by the filth of the prison. He obtained the drill suit by a ruse, ironically appropriate to a priest who was distant and pompous in his youth. To make the purchase, he pretended to be a small farmer with grandiose ideas. Here, when he tries to answer the summons by the sergeant, his legs crumble beneath him, and he is subjected to the mockery of his overseer. He stands with bowed head as all of his fellow prisoners, including the pious woman, reject him or merely ignore him. When he empties the pails, he retches. Finally, he is compelled to wait, as was Christ before Pilate, until the lieutenant, taking the jefe's place, is ready to hear his case. All of this Crucifixion imagery is so explicit that it may have been one of the reasons for the Church's initially negative attitude toward this novel.

The allusions to the last events of Christ's life are scattered among details of great physical realism and acuity, concrete descriptions which give the story of the priest's plight a foothold in the tangible world. Moral vacantness (with the possibility of rebirth, however) is represented in the chapter as leprosy, as cancer, or even as Miguel's wound near his eye, which flies buzz around. Again, when the priest begins to distinguish forms in the cell, he sees heads surrounding him "like gourds." Later in the chapter, the mestizo sits sprawling in mock majesty as the flies buzz around the vomit on the floor of his cell.

Much of this realism is unified and given form by the stench of the bucket in the priest's cell and by the continual sounds of urine hitting the sides of the pail. These details are both recurring motifs which help to structure the episode and are a means of constantly reminding the priest of his common physiology with all human beings. Although he has a momentary lapse later in the novel, here the priest's act of emptying the buckets is the complete antithesis of his fastidious life at Concepción.

The imagery of leprosy and cancer is used to advantage in the chapter. The priest's numb feet resemble the appendages of lepers, and the allusion to "haunches" connotes the animal-like level to which he has descended in terms of physical comfort. In addition, a priest with leprous feet would suggest, to most Catholics, Father Damien's work among the lepers of Molokai. Whether or not Greene had this allusion in mind, he is implying that the priest's "leprosy" is balanced by a soul which is beginning to purge itself.

Cancer too is infused with a supernatural importance. The priest thinks of the man whose insides were so rotted that his family could hardly bear the *stench* of his illness. Most important, though, is the fact that the priest was able to hear the man's confession, to shrive him. With this unfortunate person, at least, salvation came in the midst of the most pronounced physical decay and suffering. Given the number of times that the priest wants to confess but cannot, the passage is crucial to an understanding of the entire book. In addition, Greene uses the lieutenant's failing attempts to destroy the tiny black insects that scurry across his page to characterize the impossibility of eradicating the Catholic Church. And finally, after the priest-protagonist is dead, another priest arrives at the end of the novel because, Greene says, in Mexico "there was no end to life."

The realistic details in this section correlate with the priest's growing resoluteness of mind. Here, he begins to combine logical reasoning with a concern for people. Coming in disguise at the beginning of the chapter, the priest does not command the same attention that he did in Maria's village during his sermon. However, he does feel a warmth which stems from communication with a "neighbor," the old man whose pitiable loss of a daughter resembles the priest's paternal situation very much. The old man's recitation seems to bring the priest's daughter closer to him, and he pictures her realistically, recalling his last sight of her by the rubbish dump.

The "miserable happiness" he feels is evidence of his new maturity, the ability to combine suffering *and* joy. Also, the priest's ruminations concerning time and pain are grounded in a new philosophical and psychological realism. He might be killed by a well-located bullet in a fraction of a second, but he wonders how long will that moment seem? In his timeless world of the prison cell, time *seems* to stretch out indefinitely. What will time seem like, he wonders, at his execution?

In the priest's dealings with the pious woman, whom he tries to save from the possible damnation awaiting those who will not recognize their faults, he reveals his as-yet-unassimilated joining of a new, emotionally fortified intellectuality with his old habit of losing the important things of life in cold logic and fine distinctions. Here, however, it is evident that a massive, heroic struggle is taking place within his soul, one that would have been impossible in his Concepción days. Throughout the chapter, the priest's theology deepens and becomes more responsive to basic human needs, cut and honed as it is upon the pious woman's wheel of wrong-headed resolution.

The priest moves from a feeling of horror (shared with the pious woman), when he realizes that love-making is going on in the crowded cell, to a feeling of empathy with at least the female in this sexual coupling. Again, startled by the old man's account of the clergy's role in his loss of Catarina, and thoroughly convinced that he *will* die in prison, the priest recovers a discarded courage and love of truth; he explains to the pious woman that the priests had *no right* to turn Catarina against her father. His announcement of his own priesthood is a way of sealing his testimony by his blood, the best type of teaching. He feels it to be his priestly duty to shake the pious woman loose from her "invincible complacency." His failure here, however, and later with Calver, does not mar his rediscovered dedication to the ministry.

The pious woman can see only brutishness in the sex act, and the priest asks her, in a moment of keen insight, what good a confession would do her in such an uncharitable state of mind. Greene then espouses a theme developed as the thesis of his novel *The Heart of the Matter:* the sinner is closer to the heart of Christianity than is the saint. The real danger of allowing the love-making to continue, the priest says, is that "we discover that our sins have so much beauty." Speaking from his experience as a spiritually and socially exalted being *who has fallen,* the priest insists that the angels who fell into Hell may have been the comeliest. He probably has in mind Lucifer's term, "light-bearer."

The priest's sincerity about helping the pious woman is seen after she has denounced him and declared that the sooner he is dead, the better. He realizes that hatred is "just a failure of imagination." Anyone, no matter how seemingly callous he is, can be pitied if we look at him closely enough. The priest's ability to feel pity (and compassion) for the pious woman marks his new sensitivity, as he tries to find the word that will unlock her emotions. On the other hand, he wonders whether he should have left her with her illusions—that is, should he have permitted her to regard him as a martyr? Seeing her closely and through understanding eyes, he realizes that, bereft of her desired vocation as a nun, the woman has had nothing in her life.

This theology of compassion is matched with the priest's commitment to speak only the truth. His life has been filled with falsity, and now, sure that he will soon be dead, he wants to explain to others who and what he is. He confesses that he is "a whiskey priest," captured because of a bottle of brandy—*but,* "pledged to truth," he rejects the traditional, sentimentalized role of a martyr (a martyr, that is, like young Juan).

This veracity adds piquancy to the priest's thoughtful compassion: in an uncompromising way, he refutes the glib irreligiosity of the man who is making love in the corner. This man equates bravery with unbelief, and the priest deflates his thesis by attacking, paradoxically, the pretentiousness of non-belief. A refusal to believe in the jefe or the prison will not make them vanish; neither will a mere denial of God bring about His non-existence.

Again, the priest is able to see that love is better than authoritarian strictures. He says that the clergy should have taught Catarina to love her father. A criminal among his brethren, he attains a feeling of companionship not possible in his days at Concepción, when parishioners kissed his glove. Waiting for the jefe, he sees his own photograph on the wall—the Concepción photograph—and he realizes that he was much further from God then, when his sins were merely venial, than he is now because, although he is undergoing a spiritual rebirth, he is still mired in spiritual and physical corruption.

One of the priest's key lessons in pity is taught to him by the lieutenant, who takes compassion on him, a desiccated convict; the lieutenant finds the priest "too old for work," and as the lieutenant gives him a five-peso piece, the price of a Mass, formal religion and the religion of the totalitarian state both become subject to the deeper religion of humanity.

All of this abstruse theology is surprisingly worked out very naturally within the framework of a prison cell, which represents the world at large. Greene states the comparison explicitly: "This place was very like the world elsewhere." The pages are filled with personalities drawn from varied segments of human nature. Several inmates make insistent, specific demands when the priest, only a man in a uniform to them, first enters the cell, and when they are given negative answers, the fumes of resentment which they give off become palpable. One young man is imprisoned for murder, and he tells a sordid tale stressing his need to defend his mother's honor. He stresses the political corruption of the jefe, who, he feels sure, put him in prison. Significantly, his act of revenge has sexual overtones, for the man whom he killed had called his mother a whore. The anecdote leads the old man to begin his recitation. Finally, the peasants do not betray the priest when they see him clearly the next morning, and their acts suggest both their loyalty and their superstition.

The lieutenant too is invested with a share of complexity in this chapter. Not only does he feel compassion for a peon who will soon be too old to work (perhaps in the vineyards of God's day laborers), but he pities even more the hostages whom he has been forced to execute. When the priest tells him his name, "Montez," and mentions that his cousin was shot at Concepción, the lieutenant quickly retorts that the killing was not *his* fault. He seems to brood over the necessity of such rigid political control and comes close, for a moment, to placing the individual over the state. The five-peso donation is the result of this transitory rebirth of conscience. The exchange between the priest and the lieutenant ends with fine irony in the lieutenant's warning: "Don't let me see your face again." Of course, the priest, by a combination of circumstances and his conscience, *will* see the lieutenant again. And he will be executed as a result.

The Power and the Glory, in other words, is not only a religious work, but it is also a novel about a man who happens to be a priest. The now-celebate priest (who once had sex, like an ordinary man) wonders if he is guilty because he loves the product of his sin, his daughter. How is one to feel contrition for an act, no matter how grievously wrong, which has given rise to a human being? Also, the priest is trapped by theology when thinking of a possible future. How terrible he feels it would be if the hostages to be seized were in a state of Mortal Sin, dying without confession. Again, it is so like the lost priest to announce the price of his bounty. Why, he reasons, should an informant be doomed to Hell and not enjoy the fruits of his crime even while on earth? Finally, the priest's theology leads him to look straight in the eyes of the hostages in the prison yard. To look away and feign ignorance of their presence would be a sign that they were required to suffer for him.

Chapter 4

Several days after his release from jail, the priest cautiously enters the Fellowses' now-deserted banana station; he is looking for Coral, who, he hopes, will help him cross the mountains (some twenty miles away) before the rains make the journey impossible. He hopes to reach a Mexican state where religion is still practiced and tolerated to an extent, although *technically,* each ceremony will still be penalized with a nominal fine.

At the banana station, the priest finds only an injured, starving dog, and ravenous himself, he manages to trick the animal out of a bone that has a scrap or two of meat on it.

He goes onward and after a day's journey, he meets an Indian woman and, for a moment, he holds her dying baby. Apparently, the little boy was shot by soldiers; seemingly, too, Coral was either killed in the same manner or was shot when the banana station was (presumably) raided. However, these possibilities remain ambiguous. We never discover how Coral Fellows died.

The priest then accompanies the Indian woman, who has strapped her dead baby on her back, on a two days' journey until they reach a "grove of crosses," where she blesses the tiny body and leaves it at the foot of a cross, a lump of sugar near the baby's mouth. The priest wanders on then, feverish and disoriented, until he is met by a man who guides him to a large white building in the distance—a church.

Immediately, we see that this chapter is subtly tied to the preceding sections of the novel. Once again, time is not measured chronologically; here, it is measured by the ubiquitous rain clouds that threaten to make the priest's escape impossible. When the priest returns to the banana plantation, he does not know precisely how much time has elapsed since his last visit; he recalls only that the rains were some distance away. Now he knows that he has only a week left to cross the mountains.

The storm breaks, and the rain resembles sheets of drenching water; earlier, it fell "like nails" in the priest's coffin as he sat drinking the illegal spirits with the Governor's cousin and two other men. In this chapter, as the priest rushes into the shelter of a hut, he realizes instinctively that he will find nothing. In the distance, ironically, are the mountains—only twenty miles away. The priest's plight suggests Moses' view of the Promised Land, a country which he was forbidden to enter.

A number of parallels between this chapter and the overall novel center upon Coral, who, unbeknownst to the priest, is now dead. He recalls that Coral asked him to use Morse code if he returned to her home, and the priest's thought of her window recalls his brief moment of horror when he misinterpreted Coral's instructions, thinking that she might be awaiting a boyfriend who would be admitted on signal.

He realizes in this chapter how much his hopes (like her parents) have depended on Coral; he believes that she is the only one who can help him without endangering herself. In other words, without knowing it, the priest has been pinning his hopes on a dead person. The reader can see clearly the depth of his entrapment.

Symbolically, Coral's discarded essay on the American Revolution contrasts with Mexico's torpid government, which in a sense "taxes" people without their being represented. And Coral's poetry book, which is about "jewels," typifies, antithetically, the barrenness of the girl's life. The book has a blurred coat of arms, an irrelevant Latin motto, and the stamped signature of the persistent Beckley, who symbolizes in *The Power and the Glory* the impersonality of written communications. Coral's name takes on a high significance as the priest relates it to the adornments given to girls after their First Communion. Ironically, Coral *never* enjoys "communion" with her parents, and she comes close to only one valid "communication"—that is, her communication/communion with the "celebrant," the fugitive priest.

The poetry in Coral's book consists of verses which are as opaque as Coral's character; the vocabulary is arcane and archaic: the "words . . . were like Esperanto." The poetry is a sharp contrast to the priest's heartfelt description of the world, a description which led his companions in the hotel room to refer to him as "a poet." One of the verses does, however, expose a father's fervent wish to regain his daughter, and his promise to forgive "the Highland Chief." Throughout, the priest's true grief is contrasted with the glib sentimentality of the anthologized poetry.

Other tie-ins in the chapter are less obvious. For example, the priest enters the station as he left it, in darkness. As he battles the mongrel, he flaps his hands to drive it away, his gestures recalling the description of vultures throughout the novel. The dog's yellow eyes are like the mestizo's; the bitch, like the half-caste, is unable to do anything but endure the blows which the priest levels upon her back. The priest receives "communion," in a symbolic sense, as he tears the meat from the dog's bone, and the previous description of his stale breath is recalled. Once again, the priest enters a hut, which houses a pile of maize and a rat, and the temporary shelter recalls his visit to the tiny village (where Maria lives), where he was forced to hear a myriad of confessions despite his exhaustion. The Indian's face at the window, in its ignorance and vulgar determination, seems like something out of the Stone Age, suggesting a previous description of the prehistoric nature of Tench's dentistry tools.

When the mother and the priest reach the burial ground, the superstitious woman presses her dead son's innocent loins against a cross in the clear view of the *un*chaste priest. Finally, as the priest reaches safety, he rests his shoulder blades against the church; this action binds him to the now-dead Coral, who wearily rested her shoulders in the same manner, and thus it foreshadows the priest's own death. It also suggests that he is placing his trust in a false hope – namely, conventional Christianity.

The priest's confrontation with the dog is at the center of the chapter, and it is essentially a microcosm of the novel. The dog resembles the priest even physically, for it drags itself from one place to another and, with her wounded back, she suggests the load which the priest must bear in his *Via Crucis* through Mexico. Also, the bitch is like a fossil, with her ribs qualifying her for an exhibit of prehistoric artifacts. Like the priest, she has not eaten in a long time, and like many characters in the novel, she has been abandoned. But in contrast to the priest, with his human ability to feel despair, the dog blindly hopes for life. Yet, like the peasants, and like the priest at times, the dog yearns for past prosperity. She believes that her howling and her empty mimicry of the watchdog will bring back Coral and her family.

The dog's stolid and wrong-headed determination resembles that of the Indian woman, and Greene, in addition, juxtaposes his description of the dog guarding the bone with the desiccated face of the male Indian outside the mosquito wire: both are consumed with dryness. The dog threatens *between her teeth,* as do other false "communicants" in the novel; the sound is like "hate on a deathbed," foreshadowing the dying Calver's offer of a (non-existent) gun and knife to the priest, who has returned to hear his confession. Gleaming in the dog's eyes are "hunger and hope and hatred," and with these three nouns, Greene encapsulates many of the novel's themes.

The dog symbolically becomes the altar "boy" or acolyte for the priest as he uses a Latin expression from the Mass to trick the animal into giving up the sacrificial bone. The bone takes on connotations of an altar stone or relic, and the priest's sudden, evasive twist suggests a celebrant's quick motion in front of a congregation. The near-rancid but still fulsome meat, swarming with flies, is literally a bone of contention, to which the dog, the priest, and the Indian man aspire. Besides showing the depth to which the clergyman has sunk, the episode also typifies the way in which the priest probably treated his congregation when he lived in Concepción. Stealthily, he holds the bitch back with a vegetable rack and then trickily extricates the bone from her feeble grasp.

The dog is also related to Greene's description of the Indian woman guarding the child. Her anxiety for her baby resembles the dog's, as her eyes follow the priest's every movement – keeping at a distance the entire time. Like an animal, she rests on her haunches, ready to rend him with her teeth at the first indication that he might harm her child. And before he tells her that he is a priest, she approaches him in a sinister way, just skirting the ground.

The priest's battle with the dog for the bone both parallels, and contrasts with, his alcoholism and his illicit sex act with Maria: he is *still unable* to control himself. Despite mentally marking off a place on the bone where he will cease to devour the meat and thus leave some for the animal, he cannot resist the temptation to finish gnawing *all* the scraps of meat off the bone. And after he eats even the knuckle of meat near the joint, he drops only a stripped bone for the dog. Interestingly, his hunger increases with each bite, as the nausea which resulted from a completely empty stomach wears off. In terms of alcoholism, one drink did indeed lead to another, though in this episode the priest's culpability is certainly limited by his extreme physical condition.

Even so, Greene calls attention to this failure of will when the priest takes the lump of sugar from in front of the dead Indian child's mouth. He even returns to the burial site, chastising himself for abandoning the mother, and he attributes his irresponsibility to his whiskey habit. Ironically, the Indian mother is gone when he arrives, and so he succumbs to the temptation to pilfer the lump of sugar lying beside the child's mouth.

The priest's refusal to allow the starving dog even a morsel and his theft of an essential part of the child's burial rites are severe lapses in his spiritual reawakening. In this chapter, both acts are fortified by the priest's habit of specious rationalizing. As he continues to gnaw meat from the bone, he reasons (with some validity) that what he previously considered hunger was really nausea; now he must appease a valid sensation.

He reasons, too, that since the dog has sharp teeth, it will be able to eat the bone itself, a gross simplification. As the priest takes the sugar, he rationalizes that the same God who could resurrect the dead could certainly provide sustenance. For a moment, this desperate logic assuages the shame which he feels when he robs a dead baby who cannot even growl back, as did the hungry dog.

The loneliness and the abandonment felt by the priest as he stands atop the mountain alongside the deserted dead child are themes seen in this chapter as well as in the entire work. The banana station has been abandoned, and Mrs. Fellows' prediction of the family's "lost" nature has been fulfilled in a way which she could not have guessed. The priest feels that he is in Limbo, a place for lost beings who are not whole, not defined. This twilight state, he reasons, began in prison while the old man who was punished by the clergy rested his head upon the priest's shoulder. Neither good enough for salvation nor evil enough for complete damnation, the lonely priest must reach out for any straw which might float his way in the sopping environment of the banana station. In his isolation, he becomes the existential wanderer who continues the trek, all the while suspecting that he will find "nothing."

After the priest devours the sugar, with its color suggestive of the Eucharist (the bread/wafer used in Mass), he realizes that he will not see the placid, stony face of the Indian woman again. All forms of life, from reptiles to higher animals, seem to be forsaking the priest; he realizes that he is left with nothing but his breath, the word itself suggesting in this context his life spirit.

The priest's isolation from human communion is fortified by references in the chapter to things which are empty or useless. On the Fellowses' plantation, everything has been taken away except "the useless or the broken." A cardboard box is filled with scraps of paper. The small chair, which is missing a leg, cannot rock back and forth as do the chairs of the Mexican women that tilt toward the family pictures, evoking memories of better days. A nail is lodged nakedly and alone in a whitewashed wall and suggests a crucifixion. No mirror or picture hangs from it, however, like the photographs of Calver and the priest that hang from the wall of the police station. The absence of a mirror prevents the priest from fully "seeing" himself. And it is fitting that a fugitive with wounded, unshod feet should find a *broken* shoehorn. Even the river which flows outside the mosquito wire is symbolically "slow and empty."

Later, as the priest carries the dead child back into the hut, the boy is described as being like a useless piece of furniture – specifically like "a chair" (another recurrent image in this novel) brought outside but quickly withdrawn "because the grass is wet."

References to water contrast with the moral sterility and torpor (pictured in the chapter), which end in false hope. Although the priest crosses the river and emerges on the other side dripping wet, he is not symbolically purified by the water; the crossing does not signal the start of a new life. The movement of the "slow and empty" river resembles the movements of the starving, abandoned dog, which drags itself across the floor with a "wet noise." This idea of contaminated water also appeared in two of Coral's poems. The first deals with the eternal nature of a river, but is written in grandiose and stereotypical poetic diction; the second poem, with the river symbolizing a means of separation between father and daughter, is an obvious parallel to the priest's own situation.

In the first poem, the two birds are symbolic. The "coot" is an awkward duck-like bird that cannot fly very far or very fast; it is not a game bird at all. "Hern" is short for heron, a bird which lives near the water and feeds on fish; it is a bird often used in a sacramental context – for example, in poems by Hopkins and in the poems of Dylan Thomas. The coot mirrors the priest's broken-winged attempts at flight, and the hern suggests that he is the caught fish, the fish itself being a universal symbol of Christ. The term "bicker" suggests the sometimes querulous nature of the priest's confrontation. In the second poem, the "stormy water" correlates with the passionate bursts of love and need which characterize the priest's relationship with his distant daughter.

The rains subside at last, and the priest can hear the quiet patter of the raindrops, but he is not at peace. He is still bereft of human company. And soon the rains return, forming a wall as impenetrable as the language barrier between the priest and the one person whom he has managed to communicate with in this seemingly godforsaken country – the Indian woman. This second squall comes after the mother murmurs the word "church," the only reality which the priest and the woman share.

Much of the priest's journey is described, once again, in Christocentric symbols. The tiny Indian baby, whom the priest fails to save with his blend of deficient Christianity and homespun medicine, has been shot three times. The baby becomes a martyr to national exigencies, which place the capture of the guilty over the lives of the innocent. The Indian mother is "crucified" in her tireless march with her dead child slung over her back. As they approach the burial mound, the priest and the woman are seen as a kind of reverse Adam and Eve, the last survivors of a dying world, not its first inhabitants.

The evening star lights their way, and this macabre equivalent of the Star of Bethlehem shines upon the plateau of crosses, the first public symbol of Christianity that the priest has seen in many years. The star, however, does not lead to hope but to a scene in which the crosses manifest a defunct Christianity, composed of superstition and its objectification, trees which have been "left to seed." In this episode, Greene reverses the adage that faith can move mountains — or perhaps restore life on mountain plateaus. The star, like the priest's salvation, seems almost within his grasp, as it hangs low over the plain.

The priest's torments resemble Christ's under the Crown of Thorns, and his head aches as though a "stiff hat-rim" were pressing upon his forehead. He feels a great thirst, and as at Christ's death, the sky blackens suddenly and then a great deluge of water drenches everything. But, again, the water brings no relief: it streams upon the dead child as upon a pile of dung.

The chapter, then, centers on death, and at its center is the parallel between Coral's death and the death of the little Indian boy. Seeing the emptiness of Coral's room, with its wastepaper box and other depleted remnants, the priest has a premonition of death. Coral's loss is all the greater — although, of course, he does not know for a certainty that she is dead — for he remembers how this "adopted" daughter vowed to protect him against all enemies, and he remembers that he last saw his indignant and seemingly already corrupted natural daughter standing by a rubbish dump. Later, he came upon the dying, wounded baby in a darkened hut. When he felt the outline of the child's face, he was horrified to think that once again violence had triumphed. The boy was dying not of a medical disease, but of a malady closer to the heart of human nature, man's capacity for senseless destruction.

The Indian woman kisses the priest's hand, much as the priest's old parishioners once did, but now he cannot provide comfort. In death, the three-year-old child's eyes take on the yellow coloring which has been associated with contagion throughout the novel. The comparison of the dead eyes to "marbles in a solitare-board" probably contains a play upon the word "solitary" and thus fits into the chapter's theme of isolation.

In response to the woman's pleas, the priest says a prayer over the dead body – in contrast to Padre José, who refused to pray for the small, dead Anita. Yet he is convinced that the prayer will be futile, for, he muses, what good are the words of a fallen priest? Here, he experiences the same spiritual aridity that will mark even the few moments before his own death. He is unable to infuse his soul or his emotions into his words; he feels that he is contributing merely a "pious aspiration," a rehearsing of stereotyped phrases. The dead child, with his stoic mother, typifies a defunct faith, one dependent upon the superstitious notion that resurrection comes from pressing a corpse against a crooked and uneven cross. Greene permits the woman to murmur merely *"Iglesia"* (church) as a response to her son's tragic death.

All of the events in the chapter are made even more terrifying by Greene's use of time, which has become endless and elastic, without beginning and seemingly without end for the fugitive priest. It might be early in the morning when the priest arrives at the banana station – or late; he simply does not know.

As is usual in Greene's writing, philosophy is grounded upon a firm base of literary realism; in this chapter, the priest's excessive moralizing and the ugly, explicit epithets which he hurls at the dog who challenges him for a bone add to his portraiture. Also, these negative sides of his character partially insure the "alienation" of the reader, a term for the technique which prevents the audience from becoming too involved with the plight of the protagonist, from feeling too much sympathy for him, or identifying with him. Greene uses "alienation" when he wants the audience to intellectually consider the issues involved and not merely to experience pity or terror. In the chapter, the priest's covetous spirit causes him to erupt in a flood of profanities ("popular expressions picked up beside bandstands") at the old and starving dog.

Greene neatly summarizes this lost world of dead children, of a priest who fights with a dog for a bone, of weird crosses on a blackened plateau, and of fever and futility, with one significant phrase: "It was as if man in all this state had been left to man."

PART THREE

Chapter 1

This chapter is a romantic idyll in the midst of the priest's harrowing, ambiguous quest for self-reform. Accordingly, Greene's description of the Lehrs' house suggests the dreamlike, transitory nature of the priest's stay in this oasis of "the good life." The details used to depict the Lehr family are diametrically opposed to those of the preceding chapters, and the priest's reaction to the Lehrs reveals several previously undeveloped aspects of his character.

In the Lehrs' house, all news is outdated, contrasting with the imminence of the priest's flight. Mr. Lehr scans a three-week-old New York magazine which contains pictures of legislators whose well-stuffed and clean-shaven faces suggest the priest's former years. Even the pages of the magazine are clean and crackling; Lehr leafs through it as he gazes at his mountain pasture, whose grasses sway in the wind. Nearby, a tulipan tree blossoms.

In this Mexican Shangri-La, priests are virtually inviolate, although they might incur a slight fine for dispensing the sacraments. One priest, however, committed an offense apparently so heinous that he was jailed for a week. The fugitive priest cannot help but contrast the sordid idea of prison with the peace and gentleness of this "nearly free" state. The village, however, is not wholly immune from moral decay. As he haggles over the price of brandy with the wine seller, the priest wonders whether the old life in the forbidden state was not better, that perhaps "fear and death were not the worst things."

Greene suggests that the superficiality of the Lehrs and of their fellow townsmen is ultimately more destructive than the visible wickedness of the Judas-like mestizo. In fact, the priest's vision of the hypocrisy surrounding him in the town forms part of his motivation for returning with the half-caste to certain imprisonment and death.

Miss Lehr becomes Greene's embodiment of the superficial life. Although she means well, note how mechanically and tritely she speaks as she heads for the stream, asking her brother for the thousandth time how cool or warm the water is. Greene calls attention to her "shortsightedness," as she peers at the ground while padding across the grass for her "cleansing." Later, she recounts her feelings of horror and uncleanness when she accidentally came upon a copy of *Police News*. She says firmly, however, that the sordid accounts "opened my eyes" (about how evil the world really was). She feels guilty, however, because she *read* about "the other side of life," and she does not dare tell her brother about her slight "loss of innocence." She becomes the spokesman in this novel for the unexamined life, and thus, she is a prime target for Greene's dissecting comment: "It is knowing, isn't it . . . ?"

So attentive is Miss Lehr to appearances that she is upset when the priest arises too early and sees her wearing a hairnet. Later, she declares that there is probably *no harm* in a peasant kneeling to a priest, although she notes that her brother frowns upon such subservience. As she delicately and calmly wraps the priest's sandwiches in grease-proof paper for his trip, she resembles a figure from a dream, having a "curious effect of unreality." The message from the mestizo wakes the priest from his preoccupation with the "promised land" of Las Casas, and so he goes off, allowing Miss Lehr to believe that he will return. This conventional world no longer attracts him.

With his half-formed concept of Catholic ritual, Mr. Lehr, who lightly ridicules what he has made no attempt to understand, is clearly kin to his unthinking sister. In a masterful stroke, Greene puts him to sleep halfway through the chapter, and his physical lethargy correlates with his spiritual apathy. Significantly, he is sleeping when the priest leaves to set out for what will be a journey to his subsequent death.

With a weary phrase or a gesture, Lehr dismisses ideas which the priest has lived with in a very visceral way, theological concepts which have, in fact, driven him to near-madness. The holes which Miss Lehr looks for in her brother's stockings symbolize chinks in the coldly idealistic armor that he has placed between himself and the vast world of emotion.

Lehr's comments about Catholicism are stereotyped, common to those who criticize Church practices without examining their bases. Before, Greene examined the pietism and morbidity of Catholics; now he turns his attention to Lutherans. Lehr's comment concerning Church luxury and the starving parishioners is hackneyed – but effective. It irritates the priest. He carps, as does the schoolmaster, on the priest's money collections, and he fails to connect his dilapidated condition with his ideas of clerical munificence. In discussing the Gideon Bible left for salesmen, Lehr mutters the commonplace that Catholics do not read the Scriptures. More dead than alive, Lehr ironically resembles an etched figure of a bishop on a burial monument. It is no wonder that the priest does not bother to disturb him before he sets out on his journey.

Resembling Captain Fellows so closely, Lehr does not exhibit curiosity even about human affairs which are close to him. He never asks how the priest came to be rescued by his foreman. He censures Senator Hiram Long for the most pragmatic of reasons: his caustic comments might cause trouble abroad. In a key episode, he insists that the bedroom door be closed so that the priest might not accidentally glimpse Miss Lehr bathing—at quite a distance from the house. In fact, the two men cannot leave the room until Lehr's sister returns from her bath.

Lehr "allows" tiny fish to tug at his breasts as he bathes himself; this slight permissiveness is a contrast to the priest's total giving of himself. The Lehrs' Bible, with its glib moral slogans for businessmen, is as mechanical as any of the indulgence *mythos* of Catholics. Although Lehr's bedroom is monastic—like the lieutenant's—it is scarcely Christian, and the absence of a cross symbolizes more than an aversion to the physical object. The Bible, Lehr says, was used by Miss Lehr in a hotel which she once operated. This background helps to account for the cooly efficient charity which she extends to the priest.

Finally, Greene uses the schoolmaster to depict the surface quality of the totalitarian state. He is simply a bureaucrat, a law-and-order man, who repeats maxims noised about by the government. Even the mestizo sees through the superficiality of this teacher who has nothing important to say; he judges him to be a "bad man."

Forced to choose between the cold and efficient "brave new world" of the Lehrs' pasture habitat and between the mountains and swamps of downtrodden Mexico, the priest unearths long-buried personality traits. Once again, he becomes a complex person, not merely a plaster caricature from a morality play. He nimbly rejects Lehr's castigation of the Friday fast, citing his host's Prussian background, with its need for military discipline. He is not dissuaded in his argument by the fact that Lehr left Germany to avoid army service. Quickly projecting his own shame onto the situation, he embarrassingly voices his self-detestation. Greene lets the reader know where his sympathies lie by having Lehr, shortly after the discussion of fish on Friday, tugged at by the creatures in the stream during the bathing episode.

In spite of the flawed reception, however, the priest manifests a very human desire to stay at this island of lotus-eaters. The Lehrs have rescued him. They are a family, albeit a shallow one, and during his stay, he has breathed once again the intoxicating air of his old authority.

The priest is almost seduced into returning to the old path of easy, moral blindness, and in a sense, the mestizo is the priest's means of possible salvation. He is amazed at how quickly the years of privation can be put aside by the show of respect accorded by the townspeople. In fact, Lehr's comment about Church laxity leads him to wonder at the beginning of his visit whether he might not again be "settling down to idleness." Clearly, the old voice of parish authority *has* returned to him, and he reacts as "the symbol" whom the people think he should be. He even begins to patronize them, as they haggle over the price of baptisms, resurrecting his old view that the price *must* be kept high for the sacrament to be appreciated.

The priest begins to picture himself arriving in Las Casas with respectable clothing, in garb befitting the dignity of the priesthood. Perhaps influenced by the Lehrs' home, he sees himself living in decent lodgings and settling into a more organized existence. He speaks officiously to the cantina man, who responds with that mixture of respect and flippancy that a former treasurer of the Blessed Sacrament Guild might use to a pastor. This small businessman, alternately haughty and patronizing, tries to ingratiate himself with the priest by dropping names: he asks the priest to look up a friend of his in Las Casas, another treasurer of a guild.

The old life returns most clearly when the priest is hearing confessions. He wants to tell the parishioners all that he has learned about lust and love and the true meaning of sin but, instead, he utters banalities. The coldness of his old formalism erects itself like a wall between him and the sinners in this stable/confessional, which stands near a church that resembles "a block of ice" in the darkness.

Greene's themes are carried through in this chapter by reference to shoes, to the priest's recurrent brandy habit, to dreams, and to water. At the start, Miss Lehr's comfortable existence is signalled by her removal of her shoes as she sews her brother's stockings. When the priest realizes that he has accomplished nothing during his stay at the Lehrs' house, he looks at his host's elegant shoes, which he is now wearing. He is beginning, literally, to follow in Lehr's footsteps. Again, when voicing his lost hopes, he glances at the new shoes. Thus, the shoes become as important to the chapter as Macbeth's new, ill-fitting royal clothing: ". . . he was perpetually conscious of some friction, like that of an ill-fitting shoe." Only when the priest returns to shrive Calver can he walk "unshod" again, for then he has resumed his mission in life.

The priest's drinking brandy with the wine seller reminds him of his unworthiness as he recalls the previous brandy-drinking session with the Governor's cousin and, before that, the episode in which Maria saved his life. The brandy leaves a bad taste in his mouth, and he tries to hide the smell from Miss Lehr. So great is his need for alcohol, however, that later, he is willing to sacrifice decent clothing and a triumphal entry into Las Casas for a few bottles of brandy. The priest's alcoholism and his spiritual degeneration are explicitly yoked in this chapter, especially in his thought that he will need only three bottles of brandy – that he will be "cured" of drinking when he reaches the haven of Las Casas. But, as Greene puts it, "he knew he lied."

In this chapter, the priest's brandy leads to his increased attachment to the sexual sin of his past that sired his daughter. Under the influence of the brandy, he lovingly hugs his evil deed.

Dreams in the chapter reflect the transitory nature of the priest's peace with the Lehrs. Miss Lehr, at one point, vanishes like a dream, and at another, the priest muses that unhappiness has become so deeply ingrained in his makeup that *any* calm must be a dream. Third, the priest's nightmare of Christ relates to the dream which he had while in prison, and it mirrors his present spiritual state.

In this dream sequence, the eyes of the statue saints roll toward him and connote both classic guilt symptoms and the episode with the Indian woman on the mountain plateau. The vision of Christ as a dancing prostitute suggests that the priest has sold himself for a few words of respect in the Lehrs' town. Most important, it raises significant doubt about Christ's validity. The priest wonders if the Savior is really hollow, a sham, and he awakens with the horrifying impression that he has sold his life for false coinage. Coming out of the dream, the priest experiences what theologians call a "desolation of spirit," a state of despair in which salvation seems impossible.

In contrast to the previous locales in this novel, the Lehrs' home offers an abundance of water, which turns out, however, to be only an apparent good, not (symbolically) an agent for permanent cleansing. The priest is offered water by Miss Lehr and is bemused by her assertion that it need not be boiled. The priest drinks fully, and, for one of the few times in the book, he is no longer thirsty. He docilely follows his benefactor, the water-dispensing Mr. Lehr, into the bedroom to change. An aspect of the priest's peasant nature emerges when he wonders why so much ado is made about bathing: to him, sweat seems to cleanse just as well.

Water, then, does not *always* purify, and pseudo-purification becomes an important theme in the chapter. The priest muses that the Germans place cleanliness, not purity, next to godliness. Accordingly, Miss Lehr's shock over the stories in *Police News* proceeds more from prudish pietism than from true conviction, and note that despite all of his soaping, Lehr remains a superficial person.

As usual, the individual chapter here is related to the overall novel by a number of striking parallels. The Lehrs exist, as do the Fellowses, by refusing to recognize the existence of unpleasant things. Like Mrs. Fellows, Miss Lehr preserves her existence by simply ducking out of sight. As she shows the priest to the door, she keeps herself hidden from the outside world by standing behind him.

The priest's attack upon the surface faith of a woman penitent recalls his treatment of the pious woman in jail. The women respond with the same angry hauteur, proudly citing their unstinting belief in God. Both expect to gain Heaven by adhering to the prehistoric relics of Catholic *forms.*

Other parallels are briefer, but they also add strength to the novel's structure. A man named Pedro appears in this chapter, and one is reminded of the other people named Pedro, or Peter, in the work. The priest hears confessions in a barn, as he did in a previous village. With a mouth dry from brandy, the priest reflects that he is merely a play actor, reminding one, again, of young Juan. Again, Las Casas is said to have electric lights, a contrast to Greene's previous description of lamps strung together above a tiny plaza. Moreover, the mestizo brings up a matter which has been on the priest's mind: the half-caste could indeed use the reward money because of his dire poverty.

Significant too is the piece of paper which summons the priest to Calver. As did the scrap of paper from Concepción that the priest

dropped at Padre José's wall, Calver's messa
controvertible influence of the past upon th
The fragment, with its childish scrawl on
homework and, in its allusion to the indecisi.
the priest's own dilemma. Calver's exclamation, ⌐
father," confirms the motivation for the priest's return. The ⌐
in Christ's name, die – at last having fulfilled the role of "father. ⌐
summons comes as a natural culmination of all the priest's woes, and
when he decides to answer it, he feels true peace for the first time
in the novel.

At any rate, how could the priest have gone to Las Casas and confessed to his bishop that he allowed a man to die in Mortal Sin by not hearing his confession? He is trapped by his virtuous sense of duty. The mestizo's gibes play only a minor part in the priest's almost sublime, even though transitory, vision of eternity.

In keeping with the priest's decision to fulfill his office – no matter what the consequences – the Christocentric allusions in the chapter are meant primarily to define the protagonist's heroism, not to parody him. The priest periodically sees through the Lehrs' false Eden; at one point he asks his host whether there are snakes on the property. In addition, the church ruin resembles Dante's picture of ultimate Hell, combining ice with consuming fire. Like Christ, the priest operates once again in a stable, even though his counsels are a failure. The Indians' gestures while blessing themselves are similar to a priest's imposition of hands to anoint the dying in Extreme Unction, now called in Catholic liturgy the Sacrament of the Sick.

Last and perhaps most significant of the symbols in this chapter is the bit of song that the priest recalls: "I found a rose in my field." The rose is a common Spanish symbol for Christ, whom the priest has rediscovered by looking into himself. As he reverses direction, walking by the sterile, whitewashed church, the sun shines blindingly, lighting the way as a sign to the priest's destiny.

Chapter 2

After seven hours on the road and after drinking some brandy, the priest and the mestizo approach the hut where Calver, the American, is supposed to be dying. He is inside. He refuses to confess to the priest, but he admits that he *may* have wanted to do so when he wrote the note. Instead, Calver now has other things on his mind:

nts the priest to accept his gun and knife. We realize – at the e time Calver realizes – that he has neither; probably the Mexican ice took them away from him. His offer, then, can be interpreted ither as a genuine desire to see the protagonist escape, or merely as Calver's wish to kill his enemies vicariously through the priest. In this scene, Calver utters one significant half-statement. Note that in his dialogue with the priest, he hints that perhaps he didn't know about the soldiers' trap: he tells the priest, "I didn't know. . . ."

At this point, of course, the matter is of no real consequence, for the chapter itself focuses upon the priest's consumption of brandy and, as a result, the priest's inability to hear Calver's confession properly. Once again, the priest's addiction to liquor damns him.

Before drinking the brandy, the priest seemed to be a changed man – he was charitable and even careless of his personal safety in the context of his greater calling. After the brandy, however, he returns to his old testy, formalistic ways, and he is partly to blame for Calver's rejection of the last rites.

At the beginning of the chapter, the priest's carefree attitude can be seen most clearly in his dealings with the mestizo. He tells the half-caste to return the mules; he is absolutely convinced that he is likely to be ambushed, shot, or arrested. He will have no need for mules, he says, and then he fulfills the terms of his contract, giving the mestizo forty pesos (symbolically, forty pieces of silver) for the once-proposed six-day trip to Las Casas. Then he warns the mestizo to flee the place. Perhaps he does this because he remembers that another person (another "innocent," as it were), the little Indian boy, died because of Calver.

The priest is as understanding of the mestizo, whom he believes has betrayed him, as Christ was of Judas, who betrayed him. Here, the priest reaffirms his earlier position that the mestizo "isn't really bad," and then he teases him in a brief interlude of friendly bantering.

Mildly taunting the perpetually whining mestizo, the priest asks him, "Can I do nothing right?" The query is made in response to the half-caste's charge that the priest cannot do "anything in moderation." Then the priest asks the mestizo whether the guards will let him see Calver. The half-caste blurts out, "Of course . . ." without thinking. His hand is tipped.

By using this verbal trick with the mestizo, a trick that is analogous to the card tricks that he wanted to perform earlier in the novel, the priest confirms that the police are indeed awaiting him, and it is then that he takes the brandy to steady his nerves.

The two men finish the bottle of brandy, even though the priest ignores a warning with which he has reminded himself throughout the novel: a man must not drink alcohol quickly unless he has food in his stomach, and he should never drink in hot weather. Then, in an appropriate analogy, one foreshadowing the priest's execution by gunfire, the empty bottle is thrown against a rock, and the explosion, Greene says, is like shrapnel. The half-caste urges caution; people might think the priest has a gun.

Perhaps in response to Calver's telling the priest several times to "Beat it," the priest begins to treat Calver with the same mixture of sanctimonious patronization, superciliousness, and impatience that he used with the penitents of the Lehrs' town on another occasion when he had been drinking.

Calver is genuinely puzzled when the priest begins to hear his confession so formally, asking him in prescribed Church practice how long it has been since he has received the Sacrament. The priest clearly and censoriously intones that Calver's ten-year lapse is serious indeed. This opening comment, however, is only the beginning of his bickering with the dying American outlaw.

In many ways, Calver is the alter ego of the priest, his buried, completely physical and instinctive self; and, accordingly, the clergyman becomes furious when confronted with Calver's obstinacy. The priest's efforts to lead him back down the paths of remembered sin, to engender a budding sorrow within Calver, fail miserably. Calver's confession is, in all respects, a failure. Once again, the priest proves ineffectual, and he knows it, calling the situation "horribly unfair." Basically, the priest relies upon fear tactics rather than expressing the fulness of God's mercy to Calver. His method simply does not work with a man who is very brave, even though he is a killer.

Whatever valid gestures the priest does make in regard to Calver's salvation come too late: his contrast of the transitory nature of earthly life with the spaciousness of eternity, and his conditional absolution, given under the possibility that Calver may have repented the moment before his soul left his body, are too late.

As usual, symbols play a crucial part in this chapter. First, the mountain journey of the priest is similar to his own labyrinthine voyage through his mind and soul, with many circuitous and false

66

starts. The mestizo and the priest must travel one hour, two thousand tortuous feet down and then up a ravine in order to reach some Indian huts only two hundred yards away. Second, the sunlight is "heavy" and "stormy" when the priest attempts to shrive Calver, this atmospheric condition contrasting with the clear sunlight that marked the start of his trek away from the Lehrs'. The murky sunlight reflects the priest's brandy-blurred vision of his sacramental functions. Third, the ever-present mouth imagery throughout the novel is once again used to suggest danger, and note how Greene describes the watch tower. He says that it "gaped" over the path of the priest and the mestizo "like an upper jaw."

Finally, the confrontation of the priest and the convict, long anticipated in the novel, becomes a symbolic union of opposites — "the Power" and "the Glory" — and Greene questions which of the men is the saint. Calver's exclamation, "Bastards," is fortuitous; it helps arouse the priest's ire, probably because it recalls his own situation with his daughter, Brigitta. Also, the priest resembles Calver in that the murderer, like the clergyman, looks totally different from the picture of him that hangs in the police station. Both men have been radically changed from the arrogant, confident, and successful people that they once were, when the photographs were snapped.

Last, the priest repeatedly urges Calver to *repent,* citing the story of the "good thief." (In the Bible, one of the two thieves crucified alongside Christ repented on the cross and rebuked the "bad thief." Christ said that the "good thief" would be with Him in Paradise.) This reference to the "good thief" appeared earlier in the novel when the pious woman who was in prison at the same time that the priest was, told the story to him. The priest's awareness that, although *he* can hear Calver's confession, there will be no one to hear *his own confession,* heightens the irony of Calver's stubborn refusal to repent. Here, the priest plays the part of an ineffective Christ-figure, whose offer of Paradise was rejected by the "bad thief."

Chapter 3

The priest has been arrested, and for awhile, he and the lieutenant must sit alongside Calver's corpse while they wait for a heavy downpour to end. During that time, using a pack of cards that Mr. Lehr gave him, the priest is able to perform the card trick that he has wanted to show to someone throughout the novel — "Fly-away Jack."

Then, the priest and the lieutenant touch on a few topical issues, one of which is the protagonist's admission that *pride* has kept him in Mexico.

After the storm, the soldiers prepare to leave, and the mestizo appears, asking for the priest's blessing. The priest says that he will pray for the half-caste, but that the man cannot be blessed or have his sins forgiven until he returns the reward money (which he received for informing on the priest's whereabouts); if he does that, it will be proof that he is truly contrite.

The men enter the capital city of the province, and the lieutenant promises the priest that he will secure the services of Padre José, the married priest, for him, so that he can confess to a priest for the last time. Shortly thereafter, Luis, a boy whom we met earlier in the novel, when his mother was trying to instill in him the virtues of the saintlike young Juan, suddenly appears, admiring the lieutenant who captured the priest, and he asks the lieutenant if he has "got him."

This chapter, then, has a number of major ideas, but its primary focus is on the debate between the lieutenant and the priest, a disputation between, as it were, Caesar and God, or between State and Church. Greene skillfully maintains attention, however, and even suspense, in the midst of abstractions and esoteric, theological arguments. During the chapter, the priest frequently alienates the lieutenant, just as he has inadvertently done to several of the other characters in the novel. For example, he tells the lieutenant how popular his card tricks were with the Church guilds, forgetting the lieutenant's hatred for such religious organizations. The priest, however, realizes only that he has had virtually no conversation with anyone, except Mexican peasants and Indians, in the past eight years. Therefore, he simply does not know what tone to adopt when speaking to this police official.

As a result, the priest is unable to grasp all that the lieutenant is saying, although Greene does make their debate central to the novel. In addition, he allows the priest's fear of his approaching death, with its possible great pain, to blur and ignore some of the theological subtleties that could have been explored. Realistically, the priest fears the bullets almost as much as a possibly unhappy afterlife, and this very natural reaction – the fear of the impending firing squad – firmly anchors the chapter's thesis in reality and not in mere verbal gymnastics.

Note that when the priest tells the lieutenant that a little pain is nothing to dread, and when the lieutenant points out that his prisoner's hands are trembling, the priest answers that only a saint can weigh this life with its troubles against the next, and that he is *not* a saint. Greene's central thesis, enunciated by this priest, a man who is not able to practice what he preaches, lends a plausibility to a view that sacramental authority resides in the office—if not primarily in the person. Within the priest rests the power of Rome, even though he himself is, as a man, nameless and a sinner.

Greene also makes concrete the occasional flashes of insight which reveal the priest's determination *not* to relinquish even a fragment of his beliefs. The lieutenant tells the priest that, once, he wanted to give "the whole world" to the people of Mexico, to *exactly* the kind of men whom he was forced to take as hostages *because of the priest*. The priest answers simply, "Perhaps that's what you did"—that is, perhaps the lieutenant gave the hostages Life Everlasting, which would be, for the priest, "the whole world."

In addition, the lieutenant's reactions also form a solid, realistic base for the debate. Furious at one point that the priest will get his "wish" to die a martyr, he finally realizes, along with the priest, that neither of them is such a bad person after all. In fact, the debate ends by augmenting the lieutenant's humanization; he promises to seek out Padre José to hear the priest's last confession.

In this scene, the lieutenant's men also add a measure of reality; in particular, they add a sense of physical place to the debate in the tent as they constantly walk by, look in, stare curiously at the participants, and wonder if there is trouble. In general, their spontaneous actions reflect the ebb and flow of the conversation between the priest and the lieutenant. In their debate, the lieutenant supplies some of the reasons that the government has been able to implement its anticlericism; the debate also provides a good basis for understanding the total Mexican situation.

The lieutenant pictures the outlawed Church as not being pristine—in fact, as having sponsored a spy network of religious persecution, in which one villager might be encouraged to inform on another less "holy" citizen—a system presided over by a clergyman who took note of who made their Easter duty and who missed the sacraments. Furthermore, the lieutenant points out, the sins of the most corrupt landowners (even murder) were forgiven by a glib dispensation in

Confession, and the confessor (the priest) was obligated to "forget" whatever he heard during this sacrament of penance. Because of this seal of confession, then, priests were essentially prohibited from all social involvement. The lieutenant says further that he himself must respond with all of his emotions in the cause of a greater and happier nation – one no longer infested by clergymen who have to be hunted down and eradicated.

The positive view of the essential Church, presented by the priest, embodies Greene's view that the Catholic religion *will survive* all adversities caused by the overzealousness and ignorance of both those who would save it *and* those who would destroy it. For his part, the priest deftly avoids discussing specific ecclesiastical abuses. For example, he points out that in the lieutenant's perfect State, the burden of censorship will simply shift from the clergy to the police, and he cleverly argues that authority must be invested in the institution, *not* in the individual. What will happen, he asks, when the present leaders of the revolution are dead, their places taken by corrupt followers?

The lieutenant's admission – that incompetents like the jefe will always exist – does little to deny the main thrust of the priest's thesis. The priest can hear confessions and dispense the Holy Eucharist *even though* he is a drunk, a lecher, and a coward. But what base of power do the State's officials operate from? The priest makes his points even clearer when he asks for Padre José to hear his last confession. This Catholic priest, speaking for the Church, believes as his Church has taught him: a priest, even a priest like Padre José, retains the power of the priest *despite* the shambles of his personal existence.

The priest dwells on the boundlessness of God's love; to him, God's love is the major proof of the sterility of a state which rationalizes miracles and claims that God's Providence can be explained away by man's expanded consciousness. Greene portrays the State's ideal of perfection as a part-for-part harmony, without the luster of mystery, and essentially *without love*. Dependent upon the questionable strength of character of its police, the State is terribly vulnerable to human corruption. The Church, on the other hand, often functions *through* sin and *in spite of* imperfection. Its harmony is deeper and not so brittle; in fact, it will call up yet one more nameless priest at the conclusion of this novel to fulfill the famous prophecy, "The gates of Hell shall not prevail . . ." against the Church.

Greene's point in all of this is that an organization which relies merely upon human beings misses the mark and is, by its very nature, temporal. The lieutenant, in his insistence that *his* vision of the future state will remove all pain—physical, psychological, and spiritual—is uttering the trite "Crystal Palace" thinking of the mid-nineteenth century.

Greene, through the priest, is adroit with language and logic, and this cleverness is symbolized when the priest "tricks" the lieutenant at cards. He bests him in this diversion, just as he bests him in forensics, and yet, this seeming diversion fits into the novel in many ways. The serious and somber lieutenant is defined by his opening remarks: "I don't play cards . . ." The priest assures him that he does not want a full game but merely to demonstrate a few tricks.

The three cards and the three packs suggest the Holy Trinity, in this mordantly humorous exchange, as the lieutenant is defeated by the priest's religious arguments. The search for the missing jack mirrors the lieutenant's novel-long hunt for the priest, with the name of this one trick connoting the priest's retreat, "Fly-away Jack." In addition, the Church is seen to possess two "jacks" in this novel, the second arising almost from the ashes of the first priest.

The lieutenant's reaction to the trick is spontaneous and typifies his abrupt response to anything which he cannot understand: "I suppose you tell the Indians that this is a miracle of God." He does, however, relate the cards explicitly to Greene's theory of the trickery behind some ecclesiastical practices when he speaks of them in disgust, associating them with the infamous Guilds.

Chapter 4

As he promised, the lieutenant visits Padre José and asks him to hear the priest's confession, but the padre's wife, fearing that he will lose his government pension, forbids her already fearful husband to leave. When the lieutenant returns and tells the fugitive priest that Padre José will not come to hear Confession, the priest feels a great sense of abandonment. He asks the lieutenant how long the pain of death lasts during an execution.

In this chapter, both the lieutenant and the priest are deeply dejected—the lieutenant, because he is "without a purpose" now that the chase is over; and the priest (at the dawn of his last day) because he feels that he must face God empty-handed, having accomplished nothing.

This process of deflation, of having arrived at nothingness, begins in this chapter with the lieutenant standing outside of Padre José's window, very much like someone who has come to the vestry to ask a favor, or like the fugitive priest did earlier—when he asked Padre José for protection. Mistaking the purpose of the lieutenant's errand, Padre José swears that he is innocent; he did *not* grant the request of the parents of the dead little Anita. He did *not* say a prayer at her grave.

During the scene, note that the laughing children here become an explicit parody of youngsters in confessionals, as they mock Padre José from the other side of the "grille." Padre José is once again pictured with little pink eyes, looking emptily at the stars; the stars suggest the lofty heights of his abandoned calling, and his little pink eyes suggest the physical, pig-like self-abasement of his vulgar marriage.

After refusing the lieutenant's request, Padre José says that he *will* pray for the priest, his "hand-washing" act recalling the fugitive priest's meaningless gesture toward the mestizo when he left him (although the priest, unlike Padre José here, was theologically unable to shrive the unrepentant half-caste). Padre José's fumbling with his fallen trousers are symbolically seen as his abortive dressing for a church service, again typifying his buffoonery, but his sincere sympathy for a fellow priest *does* reveal a depth of understanding hidden deep beneath terrible fear. The picture that we see of Padre José, his face pressed against the "bars" of his window, suggests that he will never leave the "prison" of his sacrilegious marriage.

The fugitive priest and the lieutenant are again paralleled, this time in Greene's allusion to a "door" which is forever sealed for both of them. After the lieutenant tears down the pictures of Calver and the priest (thus ending another motif in the novel), he wearily falls into a dream which contains elements of laughter and underscores his failure to find "a door" in a long passageway (life). The priest also dreams of a "door," in a sense—a door of communication as he attempts to open communication again by means of Morse code. The priest's "door" represents the love that the priest *should have felt* for all humanity, but which he has obsessively focused upon the narrow figure of his daughter, standing beside the rubbish dump. Thus, as we have seen, the priest has failed to love the minor characters whom he has met. His failure is, in Greene's eyes, a failure to love God, Who created *all* people in His image.

Solitude is another motif which is completed in this chapter. When the priest hears that Padre José will not come to him, he drops his head between his knees: ". . . he looked as if he had abandoned everything, and been abandoned." The lieutenant asks whether the priest might like to spend his last night in a common cell with the other prisoners, but the priest responds that he wishes to be alone. He has much thinking to do.

The priest's solitude does not help him feel perfect sorrow for his sins, and his need for Padre José suggests Greene's thesis—that is, each person has a communal responsibility. Greene is on the side of those who believe that "no man is an island." Left to himself, the priest imagines that the whole world has turned away from him, and he realizes that it would have been better to spend the final night with the other prisoners. His feeling of loneliness is shared by the lieutenant, whose universe is now completely empty, since he has captured the last active priest in Mexico.

In this chapter, the lieutenant's war between emotion and logic becomes clear. Cold reason tells him that he *must* keep his promise and find a confessor for the priest in order to make credible the work of the new state. Also, he manifests the party line by dwelling smugly and disdainfully on the word "husband" when speaking to Padre José's wife. He takes pleasure in the bantering between the married clergyman and his "housekeeper"; this scene revives his old beliefs about savage religions. But, on the other hand, the lieutenant brings the priest some brandy, offers the community of the common cell, solicitously tells the priest to attempt sleep, and, in general, he does what he can to assure his captive that his death will be speedy.

In the last paragraph of the chapter, Greene hints that the priest *might* be saved, although he is unwilling to solve the enigma of the priest's destiny for the reader. For one moment, the priest is able to transcend his fear of pain, his self-pitying tears, and even more important, his fear of damnation, which would qualify him for only *im*perfect Contrition. During that one second, he seems at last to feel perfect sorrow for his sins—that is, sorrow because he has offended God: ". . . an immense disappointment because he had to go to God empty-handed, with nothing done at all." Yet, in the next moment, he (possibly) falls prey to despair, convinced that he is not a saint, and paradoxically, he knows that it would have been so easy to have been saved. Greene undoubtedly feels that it is not the prerogative of the Christian novelist to make judgments reserved for God.

PART FOUR

The final chapter of *The Power and the Glory* offers us a *direct, last look* at most of the supporting characters in the novel — in stark contrast to the *third-hand, briefly noted* look at the main character, the priest, when he is executed (a scene narrated by Mr. Tench).

In this final chapter, Captain Fellows and Trix try to avoid the subject of their daughter's death and decide to leave her remains in Mexico and build a new life for themselves back home. Tench, meanwhile, has traveled to the capital city to treat the jefe's tooth, which has been neglected for months, and he explains to the Chief of Police that his wife (Sylvia) has written him, asking for a divorce. Tench is made physically ill by the priest's execution, and abstractedly, he delays filling the tooth as the officer waits in pain. Later in the chapter, young Luis, appalled that the lieutenant has killed a true "hero," spits on the butt of the policeman's revolver. Significantly, it is Luis who, with great caution, admits the new priest at the conclusion of the novel.

Greene's central point in this final chapter is this: life goes on, some things *do* change, and people who are dynamic enough, those who have a strong life instinct, *can* throw off their inhibitions and come to a greater understanding of the most important values in life.

For the Fellowses, for the jefe, and for Luis' mother, there is *no hope,* but for Tench and Luis, there is a slight flicker of hope. Significantly, as noted, the last events of the novel are *not* seen through the priest's eyes. The story focuses, instead, on the so-called minor characters in the novel because they are the ones who *had* a chance to be affected by the priest's presence and because they must *still* play out their roles on life's chessboard now that the priest is dead.

Mrs. Fellows is helpless, despite the letter from Norah, holding a false promise of new life. We see her covering her eyes from reality, calling for more eau-de-Cologne and trying to say nothing about Coral's death while chastising her husband, who keeps inadvertently alluding to it. Greene underlines her ignorance by having her comment on the priest's execution, "There are so many priests."

The irony here is that there *are not* "so many priests"; this priest is "the last active priest." And another irony is this: if the priest's words did not affect Mrs. Fellows' destiny, they *did* influence Coral. According to Captain Fellows, Coral talked at great length – "as if he'd told her things." Now that Coral is gone, however, Mr. and Mrs. Fellows' sense of desertion is not sufficiently strong to compel an investigation of just *what* the priest may have said. Although the two people realize that "somehow nothing is ever in its place," they are too shallow to perceive the ramifications of such a potentially profound concept.

Tench's lack of insight is not as complete. Although his vision is hampered by "spots" – caused, he maintains, by indigestion, the "veil" which he sees through does *not* block off his sight (or insight) entirely, as does the handkerchief (symbolically) over Mrs. Fellows' eyes and forehead. Tench's wife's letter arouses little emotion, but he *does* feel *great* empathy for the priest who is about to be executed. In fact, Greene gives the somewhat revitalized dentist a last look at the priest. Tench feels that the priest's execution is "like seeing a neighbor shot," and he recalls how the two men had once spoken a common language, English. Tench's sense of desertion is valid.

The figure of Tench overshadows that of the jefe, who is still complaining of his sore tooth, which apparently became infected around the time that news of the priest's existence first became known. In addition, the paragraphs centering on Tench complete the animal imagery of the novel. Greene's allusion to an "arena" oddly parallels the saintly young Juan's fate with that of the priest. Greene writes, "There was the bull dead, and there was nothing more to wait for any longer."

Young Juan's story is finished, simultaneously with the death of the priest, who differs from the lachrymose plaster saint in so many ways. Young Juan's story ends with a "heroic flurry"; in contrast, the priest is unable to walk to his death unaided, although significantly, he tries "his best." In the young Juan story, the Chief of Police is visibly moved; Tench's patient, the jefe, does not even care enough to witness the execution.

Finally, it is Luis who becomes the agent who receives the new priest, a means by which Rome can continue her ministry. And by spitting on the lieutenant's revolver butt, Luis clearly rejects both the totalitarian state and violence as a means to an end. He now knows that *he* is the only man in the house, and so, while his mother sleeps, he lets in the new priest, a tall, pale, thin man with a "sour mouth" and the now familiar "small suitcase."

STRUCTURAL DEVICES

THE COMMUNION THEME

This novel is unified partially by the failing efforts of several characters to communicate significantly with one another, and Greene uses the metaphor of the Communion of the Mass, the Eucharist, to delineate their frustrated attempts. At the beginning of the novel, the dentist Tench pours symbolic wine (brandy) for the priest to drink, as he symbolically usurps the role of celebrant. Later, the crucible which he uses in his dentistry is used to blend a cheapened quality of gold, just as the priest's chalice is symbolically defective – that is, chipped. The American outlaw, Calver, and the nameless priest exist in a mystical, parallel communion throughout *The Power and the Glory*. Both of their outdated pictures hang in the police station; the photograph of the priest is one taken at a First Communion party long ago.

Throughout the novel, Greene cites the pathos of priestly celibacy in the priest's inability to communicate truly with Maria, the mother of his child. Maria provides all of the ingredients for him to celebrate Mass, but the priest must hurry the Sacrifice because of the arrival of the police. In like manner, he is prohibited from "communicating" fully with Maria in a marriage because he is a priest.

The wine-buying episode in the hotel room exemplifies, symbolically, the priest's inability to carry out his clerical function – that is, to distribute the Eucharist. Here, the Governor's cousin and the jefe drink all of the precious wine, leaving the priest with only brandy, which is unusable in the Consecration. The priest is as ineffectual in this setting as he was years before at Concepción, and his memory constantly returns to his pompous strictures at the First Communion celebration. Later, he associates Coral Fellows' name with the gemstones worn by girls after their First Communion.

On one level, this novel traces the priest's realization that Communion, in the theological sense, is not as important as compassion and human understanding. All of this Communion symbolism is reinforced by the many references to teeth in the novel. The mouths of the characters, except for the pious woman in the jail cell, are unfit for the reception of the Eucharist.

THE CONFESSION THEME

If, as we have seen, the characters in this novel are unable to symbolically receive Communion, neither can they symbolically "confess" to one another. The Fellowses have long ago lost the ability to communicate; the mestizo threatens to use the guise of Confession to trap the priest into admitting his ministry; and the priest's death is occasioned by his return to a police state to shrive Calver.

Padre José steadfastly refuses to hear the condemned fugitive's confession, and the priest worries that hostages might be shot and die without receiving penance. Again, Greene replaces the formality of theology with the human virtue of humility. The priest-protagonist is close to God when he "confesses" that Padre José was always the better priest, even though he fails to carry out the formal Church stipulations concerning the Sacrament for the priest who is about to die.

FALSE FATHERS

False fathers permeate the novel and help to define the priest's dilemma: the emotion that he feels for Brigitta should, by Catholic precept, be applied to all the "children" of his congregation – in fact, to all the "children" (men, women, and children) in the entire country of Mexico. Other "fathers" in the book serve as foils to the priest. Padre José is an obviously ineffectual "father" (or priest); he married after government insistence, and he spends his days living with a nagging, grotesque wife. Luis' father has abdicated his responsibility; he leaves the task of rearing their three children to his wife. In short, his only contribution to the marriage is an occasional, cynical comment about traditional religion.

Coral Fellows' father is serene in his ignorance and inefficiency, and his daughter, therefore, becomes the true head of the family. Captain Fellows' negligence presses her into maturity before her time. And, in almost a parallel situation, the Tenches ceased to exchange letters after the death of their son.

The priest's guilt is heightened by Brigitta's spiritual condition; his daughter seems already condemned to a hell in both this life and in the afterlife. Fatherhood throughout the novel becomes a metaphor for the characters' inability to communicate successfully in the world of emotions and reality. Even the lieutenant is a misguided "father," wanting to spare the new children of Mexico the privations which he experienced as a child. His gospel, however, is rejected by Luis, who spits on the lieutenant's pistol at the end of the novel.

Finally, Calver also fits into this false father theme of the book. He addresses the priest as "father" in his note; then, he enrages him by using the term "bastard" to describe the police, just as the priest is trying to hear his confession.

THE LIEUTENANT AND THE PRIEST

In an essay, Greene emphasizes that the lieutenant is not all bad. Both the lieutenant and the priest are leaders of two different types of totalitarian states, and both have the good of the people at heart, although their means are diametrically opposed.

The priest's three meetings with the lieutenant correspond to Christ's three falls on His way to the Cross, and they form a major structuring device in the novel. All of the priest's meanderings seem to gravitate toward these confrontations, and the final meeting ends with a partial reconciliation of opposites. The lieutenant is able to see the worth of his prisoner, and he does all he can to comfort the priest during his last hours. This kindness is foreshadowed in the second meeting, when the lieutenant gives the disguised clergyman a five-peso note, the price of a Mass. He feels that the priest might soon be too old to work.

THE YOUNG JUAN STORY

Almost all of the priest's actions should be viewed against the backdrop of young Juan's holy doings. The priest's Way of the Cross unfolds section by section, counterpointing the mother's reading of young Juan's sentimental saga. At the end, young Juan cries out "Long live Christ the King," but the priest, in contrast, must be led to his execution because his legs are buckling beneath him.

The novel is written, in part, to refute the kind of destructive sentimentality inherent in traditional religion, the type that helped bring about persecution by the police state in the first place. Greene's book is a deliberate and vibrant protest against the tale of young Juan. His rendering of a very human priest gives lie to the plaster saint.

MOTIFS

THE BIBLICAL MOTIF

The priest's journey through Mexico is his *Via Crucis* (Way of the Cross), and the novel is filled with comparisons between the priest and Christ. The protagonist's salvation is worked out upon a "true cross," which ironically necessitates his staying away from Vera Cruz.

The priest's mission is carried on in hidden barns resembling Christ's furtive stable, which quickly became a target for Herod and his pursuers. His visit to Maria resembles Christ's sojourn at the home of Mary and Martha in Bethany.

In prison, the priest is treated like Christ on Holy Thursday night; and he is forced to empty the pails of excrement, a parallel to Christ's washing the feet of his Apostles at the Last Supper. In prison, too, he is compared to (and contrasted with) the "good thief," who repented on Good Friday.

When the priest ascends to the mountain plateau with the Indian woman, he sees only crooked crosses, illuminated by a low hanging Star of Bethlehem. Falling short of salvation, he feels that he is "crowned" with thorns as his sharp hat rim presses into his head. However, when he rides astride a donkey toward Calver, the priest for a moment feels at one with God; the snippet of his song, "I found a rose [Christ] in my field," indicates the rectitude of his choice *not* to remain in a relatively safe province.

Other biblical personages serve as well to define the protagonist and the principals of the novel. Fellows is Pilate-like in his willingness to relinquish the priest to the state – as is Padre José. Coral Fellows is crucified by coming into puberty; she wearily leans against the hot, hard wall of the banana station. Young Juan's story is a parody of the Gospel according to Saint John. The priest, unable to enter the village of his birth, is like Moses, shut out from the Promised Land. He baptizes a boy as "Brigitta" instead of "Pedro," just as he bungled his role in Peter's Church – that is, the Roman Catholic Church. The mestizo is a Judas-figure. And Calver becomes the "bad thief," more concerned with escape (albeit the priest's) than with salvation; his name, of course, suggests Calvary.

In his use of these religious symbols, Greene is a Modernist, one who employs a universally recognizable structure of myth to define contemporary individuals. While he may not accept the validity of every aspect of the theological system, he uses Scripture, as do James Joyce and T. S. Eliot, for "all it is worth." Padre José's moral cowardice, for example, becomes clearer when matched against the courage of St. Joseph, the patron saint of the Happy Family.

ANIMAL IMAGERY

On three occasions, Greene describes the priest's plight in terms of a bull who is about to be killed in an arena, and allusions to animals of all types abound on the pages of the novel. Without God, Greene implies, man is reduced to the state of the lower creatures. Buzzards flap their wings as if to toll the death knell of Mexico's police state, all the time staring on with "moron" faces. Dogs figure prominently in the novel, and during a crucial chapter, the priest battles a starving mongrel for the last bit of rancid meat on a discarded bone.

The priest is chased through the streets of the capital city like a rat through a maze by the Red Shirts, and the mestizo is compared to a bloodhound as he relentlessly stalks the clergyman. The mestizo sits in his jail cell, calling for beer as flies buzz around his vomit; and, in jail, the priest discovers that the hostage Miguel has been beaten like an animal; flies are buzzing around his wounded eye. The lieutenant tries to kill the numerous black insects that scurry across his book, but his gesture is as futile as his attempts to prevent future priests from coming into his state.

Humanity at its most abject level is seen in the hungry clergyman's treatment of the mongrel: the dog becomes an "altar boy," as the priest, using a bit of Latin from the Mass service, deceives the animal into relinquishing its hold on the bone. Ironically, Greene's theme in all of this is that man is saved *only* by recognizing and accepting his lower self: he ascends by first descending.

THE DECAY MOTIF

Greene pictures the death of Mexico under its godless government through vivid details of decay, physical sordidness, and sterility. The

General Obregon looks as though it is ready to sink, and busts of recent heroic generals are being covered quickly with mildew. As the nauseous and forgetful Tench walks toward the wharf, he spits bile into the street, becoming one of many people in the novel who express their disgust by spitting. The curfew is an artificial device to secure a moribund state against the rain and the heat, both moral and physical, which constantly threatens to engulf it. The crumbling of Mexico is seen in taxis that have no passengers, dynamos that run only haltingly and sporadically, grandmothers who rock back and forth silently, locked in the prisons of their memories, and playground swings that stand like gallows next to a ruined cathedral. The novel is saturated with the "green sour smell" of a Mexican river.

STUDY QUESTIONS AND ESSAY TOPICS

1. How does Tench's meeting with the priest establish at the outset of the novel a sense of decay and sterility?

2. How does the story of young Juan contrast with the unfolding of the priest's martyrdom?

3. How does the Fellows family manifest Greene's theme of human indifference or non-involvement?

4. In what ways is Coral Fellows the priest's spiritual daughter?

5. How is Padre José a "false father" figure? Does he have any virtues?

6. What role does the jefe play in the novel?

7. Trace several ways in which the priest and the lieutenant are alike.

8. What are Maria's motivations for protecting the priest?

9. Discuss the symbolism of the priest's wine-tasting "celebration" in the hotel room with the Governor's cousin, the beggar, and the jefe.

10. How does the priest's night in jail change his outlook on human nature?

11. In what ways is the priest's confrontation with the mongrel dog central to Greene's themes in the novel?

12. What is the importance of the priest's meeting with the Indian woman?

13. Why is the Lehrs' home a false Eden?

14. Describe the symbolism behind the priest's dreams.

15. How is the priest's charity evidenced after he decides to return to Calver?

16. How does the priest's drinking influence his dealings with Calver?

17. Summarize the debate between the priest and the lieutenant.

18. How does Greene indicate the lieutenant's charity before the priest's death?

19. Discuss Tench's sense of desertion at the end of the book.

20. Describe the significance of the arrival of the new priest at the end of the book.

SELECTED BIBLIOGRAPHY

ALLOTT, KENNETH, AND MIRIAN FARRIS. *The Art of Graham Greene.* New York: Russell & Russell, 1963. Traces balance and irony in the structure of *The Power and the Glory.*

ATKINS, JOHN ALFRED. *Graham Greene.* New York: Roy, 1957. Analysis of the role of suffering in the novel.

82

DeVitis, A. A. *Graham Greene.* New York: Twayne, 1964. Systematic treatment of all the important works.

Donaghy, Henry J. *Graham Greene: An Introduction to His Writing.* Amsterdam: Rodopi, 1983. Emphasizes Greene's realistic and plausible treatment of allegorical elements in *The Power and the Glory.*

Evans, Robert Owens, ed. *Graham Greene: Some Critical Considerations.* Lexington: University of Kentucky Press, 1963. Some excellent pieces, though others are dated.

Hynes, Samuel Lynn. *Graham Greene: A Collection of Critical Essays.* Englewood Cliffs, N.J.: Prentice-Hall, 1973. Several thoughtful pieces in this Twentieth Century Views collection.

Kunkel, Francis Leo. *The Labyrinthine Ways of Graham Greene.* New York: Sheed & Ward, 1959; Rev. ed. Mamaroneck, N.Y.: Paul P. Appel, 1973.

Lewis, R. W. B., and Peter J. Conn. *Graham Greene: The Power and the Glory: Text and Criticism.* The Viking Critical Library. New York: The Viking Press, 1970. Contains selections from Greene's writing apart from *The Power and the Glory,* an interview with Greene, and essays by leading twentieth-century critics.

Lodge, David. *Graham Greene.* New York: Columbia University Press, 1966. Solid, short work on the novelist.

Spurling, John. *Graham Greene.* London: Methuen, 1983. Short but well-reasoned study using the thematic approach to Greene's works; sees *The Power and the Glory* as one of the four first-rate works in Greene's canon.

Stratford, Philip. *Faith and Fiction, Creative Process in Greene and Mauriac.* Notre Dame, Ind.: University of Notre Dame Press, 1964. Complexity of Greene is seen in his reluctance to condemn; includes bibliography.

TURNELL, MARTIN. *Graham Greene, A Critical Essay.* Grand Rapids: Eerdmans, 1967. Good short sketch of Greene's limits as a stylist and as a theologian.

WYNDHAM, FRANCIS. *Graham Greene.* Longmans, Green, 1955. A short work, focusing on the religious sense of the novel.

VANN, JERRY DON. *Graham Greene: A Checklist of Criticism.* Kent, Ohio: Kent State University Press, 1970. Indispensable list of important critical articles.

NOTES

NOTES

NOTES

NOTES

NOTES